A Spiritual Growth Plan for Your Phlegmatic Child

Connie Rossini

Four Waters Press
NEW ULM, MINNESOTA

Cover photo by Mila Atkovska, via Shutterstock. Cover Design by Connie Rossini.

© 2015 Four Waters Press
217 South Jefferson Street
New Ulm, Minnesota 56073

Ordering Information:
Special discounts are available on large-quantity purchases by parishes, book clubs, associations, and others. For details, contact the publisher at the address above.

ISBN: 978-0-9972023-0-4

To Carlo,

my contented phlegmatic child,
with love and appreciation for your quiet gifts.

Contents

Introduction

In April 2006 our parish opened a new Adoration Chapel. My husband Dan and I signed up for the nine to ten P.M. hour on Wednesdays. We planned to take turns going to pray. On my nights, I took our newborn son Carlo with me in his car seat. That way, if he got hungry, I could quietly feed him. I wouldn't have to worry that he was crying for me at home.

The first several weeks, everything went well. Carlo was usually quiet and rarely wanted to be fed. Then one evening, he began crying. I tried to nurse him, but he did not want to eat. He was inconsolable. At last I took him out into the vestibule and walked him back and forth, patting his back. Still he did not calm down. Since two other adorers where there that night, I decided to take him home. I couldn't imagine what the problem was. He didn't feel hot. He had never been colicky.

For the next few days at home he repeated this pattern. Shortly after nine P.M. he would start crying. Suddenly I realized what was wrong. He was tired. He wanted to go to bed! My older two sons had never gone to bed with ease. In fact, my oldest rarely napped either, and was the first one up in the morning. Who would have thought I'd have a child who actually begged to be put to bed?

From then on I tucked Carlo in just before heading out to adoration. I knew he would sleep soundly for a few hours, giving me time to pray and Dan time to relax.

Carlo is my phlegmatic-sanguine child. His has been the temperament hardest for me to pin down among our four sons. Ironically, I am primarily phlegmatic myself, but I have a strong melancholic streak as well. It has taken lots of reflection and discussions with my son to determine that his primary temperament is the same as mine.

Having a child who (partly) shares my temperament has not been as easy as it might at first seem. I cannot confront his weaknesses if I am unwilling to confront my own. And I have largely forgotten what used to motivate me in childhood. I have adapted myself to others and mellowed in some ways over the years.

Recently I began using knowledge of my children's temperaments to help them grow in their relationships with each other and with God. I have taken the initiative in our home, since I am primarily responsible for homeschooling our children. My husband helps refine my understanding of the temperaments, based on training he has received at work. He supports and encourages us, without being so involved in the daily details. We include temperament studies as part of our school day. I work one on one with each child while another takes his piano lesson. During this time, we discuss any recent problems the child has had with his temperament. For the phlegmatic child, I might ask why he was willing to work so hard on one task without complaint, when other tasks are repeatedly left undone. We read short stories or portions of longer books that showcase a character's good use or misuse of his temperament.

Since beginning this venture, our relationships with each of our children, and their relationships with each other, have deepened. We are each more apt to take the other's temperament into consideration when we disagree. We are changing our expectations and our perceptions of each other. It is a long-term project, but we are all growing closer to Christ and to one another.

I would like to share some of our successes with you, so that you can use them with your children.

This book is the second full-length volume in a series of four. It follows the book on the choleric temperament, which is opposite to the phlegmatic. I hope to complete books on the remaining two temperaments soon. My primary focus in this series is to help you raise virtuous sons and daughters. I concentrate on children in elementary through junior high school, although you can adapt some of the suggestions to children who are older or younger. Lesson Plan 5 is aimed at high school students. I also have some book recommendations for phlegmatic high schoolers.

Temperaments and Spiritual Growth

God made human beings in his image, with an intellect and a will. He made us to know and love him. He calls us to serve him with both our head and our heart. Knowledge of our temperaments helps us in several ways. It shows us that our problems are not unique. We can learn from others' successes and failures. Once we know the primary strengths and weaknesses of our temperament, we can use this knowledge to grow in virtue. We can focus our energy on combating the main fault of our temperament first, leaving lesser problems for a later time. Fr. Conrad Hock writes:

> One of the most reliable means of learning to know oneself is the study of the temperaments. For if a man is fully cognizant of his temperament, he can learn easily to direct and control himself. If

he is able to discern the temperament of others, he can better understand and help them.[1]

Knowing our children's temperaments is similarly helpful. Sometimes we struggle to understand our children who have temperaments opposite to our own. When we learn about their temperaments, we not only learn to see things from their perspective, we also learn about their God-given strengths. We stop trying to remake them in our image and accept the image of God that they express through their temperament. On the other hand, recognizing that a child has a similar temperament to our own can help us watch out for problems we have struggled with. We can share what has worked for us, and what we are still trying to overcome. Whether our children are like us or completely different, we can encourage their special gifts, and share stories of saints who were like them. We thus help them become more mature Christians and more effective servants of God.

Can We Really Help our Kids Grow Spiritually?

Another Catholic writer I consulted while I was drafting the choleric book contended that it was dangerous to expect much spiritual growth out of our children. We can't expect kids to be—well, adults. If we push them too far, they might run away from the faith.

Let's think about that for a minute. Consider academic subjects. If we push kids too far in math, some of them might grow to hate it. But we still require nearly all kids to learn the basics. Then when

---

[1] Fr. Conrad Hock, *The Four Temperaments and the Spiritual Life* (Milwaukee: Pallotine Brothers, 1934), www.catholicapologetics.info/catholicteaching/virtue/temperaments.htm (accessed April 12, 2015), 1:1.

they get to senior high or beyond, they make the choice whether to continue studying math or not.

Spiritual growth is infinitely more important than mathematical knowledge. No, we shouldn't expect our first-graders to understand deep theology or be at an advanced stage of prayer. We should, however, help our children to grow up, both as humans and as Christians.

Pope St. John Paul II wrote about spiritual growth and the family:

> What is needed is a continuous, permanent conversion which, while requiring an interior detachment from every evil and an adherence to good in its fullness, is brought about concretely in steps which lead us ever forward. Thus a dynamic process develops, one which advances gradually with the progressive integration of the gifts of God and the demands of His definitive and absolute love in the entire personal and social life of man. Therefore an educational growth process is necessary, in order that individual believers, families and peoples, even civilization itself, by beginning from what they have already received of the mystery of Christ, may patiently be led forward, arriving at a richer understanding and a fuller integration of this mystery in their lives.[2]

This series is written to help families in that educational growth process, that patient leading forward of each member. Of course, we mold the religious formation to the child, his age, intellectual ability—and temperament. By focusing on temperament, I believe we do the best we can to make sure we don't push him farther than he can go. We make the faith attractive to him. We show him that we (and God) appreciate him for who he is. We give him the knowledge and the tools, and help him form the habits, that he needs to continue

---

[2] John Paul II, *Familiaris Consortio*, Apostolic Exhortation on the Role of the Christian Family in the Modern World, *Vatican Web site,* w2.vatican.va/content/john-paul-ii/en/apost_exhortations/documents/hf_jp-ii_exh_19811122_familiaris-consortio.html, (accessed April 13, 2015), no. 8.

maturing in adulthood. We cannot make him a saint, but we can show him how to begin becoming one.

How to Use this Book

Since this is the second book in a series, some of you will have already read a book on one of the other temperaments. All four books follow the same basic format. Each book contains a few basics found in all, but almost every section also contains material unique to one book.

As with the whole series, this book can be used by parents who are already well versed in the four temperaments and by those who are just learning. Some of you will appreciate philosophical grounding. I begin with an overview of the four classic temperaments in chapter 1. Chapter 2 focuses on children who have a mixed phlegmatic-sanguine or phlegmatic-melancholic temperament. Chapter 3 examines the lives of two phlegmatic characters in the Bible. Chapter 4 discusses the meaning and means of spiritual growth. In chapters 5 through 12 you'll find specific suggestions to help your child grow in prayer and virtue, along with general teaching tips for homeschoolers in chapter 9. Chapter 13 contains book lists and examples of saints and heroes who were phlegmatics. It also includes Bible verses for your child to memorize and longer portions of Scripture for him to study. Chapter 14 has detailed lesson plans for those who are in charge of their children's general or religious education. The final chapter contains the templates you need to plan your temperament studies. Feel free to use whichever parts of the book fit your needs.

For ease of reading, I use the traditional pronouns "he" and "him," et cetera, throughout most of the book. I am sure the reader will understand that I am writing for parents of both boys and girls.

Similarly, I assume that most of my audience is part of intact, two-parent, married families. I mean no offense to the widowed, divorced, or otherwise single parents among my readers, but I do not have the personal experience or expertise to fine-tune my advice to your situations. I would not want to be presumptuous. I leave the adaptation of my advice to you.

CHAPTER 1

The Phlegmatic Temperament

The Greek physician Hippocrates (from whom we get the Hippocratic Oath) first proposed the four temperaments in the fourth century B.C. He believed that bodily fluids help determine how individuals react to stimuli. Finding four basic patterns of reactions, he related them to four bodily fluids or humors, calling them choleric, sanguine, phlegmatic, and melancholic. A later physician named Galen refined this theory. Today we no longer view the temperaments as rooted in bodily fluids. However, many psychologists and Catholic theologians continue to promote the four temperament divisions Hippocrates observed.

As Hippocrates noted, some people respond to stimuli without thinking. Others need time to reflect. Some people's impressions endure. Others' impressions soon fade. Experts often call these differences "degrees of excitability." Cholerics have quick reactions and lasting impressions. Sanguines react quickly, but their feelings fade almost at once. These are the two extroverted temperaments. Phlegmatics react slowly with fading feelings. Melancholics also react slowly, but their impressions last. Phlegmatics and melancholics are introverts.

I like to think of the temperaments as four squares within a larger square. Starting with the top left and proceeding clockwise, the four temperaments are choleric, sanguine, phlegmatic, and melancholic. The two top squares are the extroverted temperaments. The two bottom squares are the introverted. The two right squares have short-lived impressions. The two left squares have long-lived.

Choleric quick reaction long-lived impression	Sanguine quick reaction short-lived impression
Melancholic slow reaction long-lived impression	Phlegmatic slow reaction short-lived impression

Does everyone have one of these temperaments?

Besides the four pure temperaments, there are also mixed temperaments. Many people are choleric-sanguine, sanguine-phlegmatic, phlegmatic-melancholic, or melancholic-choleric. Some people appear to have a few characteristics of a third temperament. Experts disagree on whether a third temperament is possible. What appears to be a third temperament could actually be habits of behavior influenced by one's environment. Most authorities agree that a healthy

person would not be evenly split between two opposite temperaments. A phlegmatic-choleric, for instance, would probably be an
unhealthy personality.

Temperaments are genetic, but that does not mean that all members of a family will have the same temperament, just as they will not
necessarily all have the same hair color. For example, my father is
sanguine-choleric and my mother is choleric-melancholic. Yet I and
most of my siblings are phlegmatic, melancholic, or a combination
of the two. Only two out of nine of us are strongly choleric. On the
other hand, I know of some families in which almost everyone has
the same temperament.

Temperament Versus Personality

Googling "temperaments" results in a host of websites with different
temperament systems. Many of these systems are broadly based on
behavior, not specifically on reaction to stimuli. They thus draw the
lines between temperaments differently than Hippocrates did. Some
of them appear to be descriptions of personalities, rather than temperaments. What is the difference? Fr. Jordan Aumann, OP, writes:

> We must ... consider the human person in terms of temperaments
> and character, which are the basic elements that constitute per-
> sonhood.... Heredity is the fundamental source of temperament,
> and environment is the basic causal factor of character.[3]

Together temperament and character create a personality. Temperament is inborn and unchangeable. Although a person can cer-
tainly learn to control his temperament (or I would not have written
this book), he can never acquire a different temperament. Personali-

---

[3] Jordan Aumann, OP, *Spiritual Theology*,
archive.org/stream/SpiritualTheologyByFr.JordanAumannO.p/AumannO.p.Spiritua
lTheologyall_djvu.txt (accessed April 12, 2015), 2:7.

ty, on the other hand, includes many factors, temperament being just one. Personality is formed by a combination of heredity, family structure, culture, health, religion, education, and habits. It develops over a lifetime as we respond to forces outside ourselves.

When considering the phlegmatic temperament in particular, we must take note of a recent adaptation of the four classic temperaments. In the 1980s a group of Christian counselors led by Richard and Phyllis Arno suggested a fifth temperament, called supine. They also redefined the meaning of the phlegmatic temperament. Some readers have told me they have been diagnosed as supine. If you are interested in the background of the supine temperament and the ways it differs from the classic phlegmatic, please see the Appendix.

How is Temperament Related to Behavior?

How do we know that the classic temperament system is more accurate than personality-based models or the Arnos' system? Can we really correlate a whole swath of behaviors with a specific type of reaction to stimuli?

We are not discussing dogma when we discuss the temperaments. There is room for disagreement. However, I have found the classic temperament divisions to work for virtually everyone who understands them and understands themselves. Here is how certain behaviors are connected to a specific temperament.

The choleric reacts quickly with strong and lasting impressions. Since his impressions last, he is determined to stick to his original way of seeing things. He does not change his perspective easily. He has a hard time letting go of arguments. His anger can be explosive and lasts a long time. He responds negatively to ideas other than his own. If he can see a way of making an idea his own, adding his input or incorporating it into his personal goals, he can then embrace it.

He learns what he really thinks by talking about it. Arguing refines his thought. Since he is outwardly focused and persistent, he has great physical energy.

The sanguine reacts strongly and at once, but is moved just as strongly by the next stimulus, and so puts the past reaction aside. He is highly distractible. He wants to move on after a disagreement and help others to do the same, so he'll urge them to overcome their differences. Since he runs from one impression to the next, he lacks commitment. He makes friends easily, but few of his friendships are deep. He does not think ahead and has a hard time learning from his mistakes. He eagerly embraces a new project, but rarely follows through to the end.

The phlegmatic reacts slowly and mildly and does not hang onto impressions. He is inwardly focused and peaceful within himself. Conflict upsets him. It moves him against his will. He acts based on how his actions will affect his and others' peace. Physical activity wears him out quickly, as does too much talking. He may even find intellectual work too taxing. He has difficulty making decisions. He is out of touch with his feelings and has trouble expressing them.

The melancholic reacts slowly, but retains his impressions. He may overlook a first offense or even a second. But by the third, his anger often boils over. He has a long memory and difficulty forgiving wrongs. He perseveres in his commitments. He takes rules seriously. He has few friendships, but they are deep. He is thoughtful and serious. He will stick with a job until it is finished, feeling that the burden to complete it is on him. He can be too hard on himself and others.

Each of the characteristics we associate with a particular temperament is a manifestation of reaction to stimuli. These reactions are inborn. However, we can learn to regulate our behavior so that we can minimize the negative behaviors associated with our temperament. We can also learn how to use our temperament for positive good.

What Distinguishes the Phlegmatic Temperament?

The pure phlegmatic temperament is usually easy to identify. As the parent of a phlegmatic child, you probably rejoiced at how easy he was as an infant. Many phlegmatic babies sleep long hours, take lots of naps, and are content in between. They give parents whose older children had stronger temperaments a pleasant surprise.

But what does this child look like as he gets older? He is content to sit and play by himself while his mother homeschools his siblings. He eats nearly everything that is set before him without complaint. He is quiet, but has a sweet smile. He is seldom defiant, but can throw temper tantrums when you suddenly change your plans. If he gets into trouble in school, it's because a friend was talking to him when they were supposed to be working. He did not want to hurt the friend by refusing to listen to him. Everyone likes the phlegmatic, yet they forget to include him in their plans. He feels overlooked and under-appreciated. He longs to be part of the group, but may be too shy to ask others if he can join them. He is loyal, traditional, conservative, and follows the rules. Fr. Aumann writes of phlegmatics, "They have good hearts, but they seem to be cold. They would sacrifice to the point of heroism if it were necessary, but they lack enthusiasm and spontaneity because they are reserved and somewhat indolent by nature."[4]

Your greatest challenge with your phlegmatic child may be motivating him to act. His reply to your directives is often, "Just a minute." He has trouble keeping his room clean. His talents sometimes

---

[4] Aumann, 2:7.

remain hidden, because he doesn't practice them. Night after night he may forget to do his homework. He'd rather stay indoors watching TV than go out and play ball. Once he gets started on a chore, he proceeds slowly. He would rather do something boring than a challenging job that doesn't suit his interests. He resists changing direction. He may "lose many good opportunities because [he] delay[s] so long in putting works into operation."[5]

He is indecisive, people-pleasing, low-key, measured, and can see everyone's viewpoint. He loves vacations and holidays, loves having a day of rest each week. He enjoys spending time with people, but he needs ample time alone too. Conflict and chaos disturb him. He'd rather cause a big problem down the road than face an argument or disappoint someone now. He is a sympathetic listener, and can have a reputation for listening to everyone else's problems while never sharing his own feelings. Sometimes his feelings are buried so deeply, he doesn't even know what they are. He remains calm under stress, as long as other people don't try to tell him to act in a certain way. He can take a long time to grow up. Late priestly or religious vocations often come from phlegmatics. He may put off going to college, getting his own place, dating, or getting married. He will stay in a dead-end job for years rather than make the move to pursue something he loves.

Some authors call the phlegmatic egotistical or selfish. I prefer to think of him as very introspective. He tends not to consider others and their problems, not because he doesn't care, but because he has to go out of his normal path of thinking to do so. When he hears about someone else who is in trouble, he is moved by compassion and wants to help at once. He lends a sympathetic ear, promises prayer and moral support, if not hard work on the other's behalf. He

---

[5] Ibid.

is fiercely loyal. While he may shrug off criticism or slights aimed at himself, he is roused to anger at the injustices done to those he loves. His defense of them may be less logical than it is affectionate. Other people are important to him, but they also trouble him, because they force him out of his ruts. They prevent him from getting the quiet and solitude he enjoys. He may not recognize how much he depends on others' friendship and love until they are gone. He can't imagine betraying a friend or family member. Sometimes his loyalty may keep him stuck in an abusive or otherwise unhealthy relationship. He can be the doormat that everyone walks over.

It's important to recall that every phlegmatic child is different. Some may have all the characteristics I've listed, others may have most. What sets the phlegmatic apart is his reaction to stimuli. Remember, the phlegmatic responds slowly and mildly to stimuli that come to him through his senses. He doesn't hold onto his impressions for long. He is generally content with the status quo.

A Quick Reference for the Phlegmatic Temperament

The phlegmatic is characterized by:
- low energy
- love for people
- need for quiet
- inertia
- desire for peace
- contentment with the status quo
- timidity
- need for affirmation
- hyper-focus on one thing
- sympathetic listening
- care for others' feelings
- objectivity

- ability to see all sides
- difficulty making decisions
- desire to help others
- tendency to be overlooked
- mild and slow reactions
- high tolerance for others' foibles
- introversion
- loyalty
- conservatism
- desire to please others
- good intentions, but little follow through
- being easily overwhelmed
- getting along with everyone
- forgetfulness
- need for support
- adherence to rules
- comfort with structure
- feeling taken advantage of
- appreciation for beauty, rather than order
- being misunderstood
- remaining calm
- predictability and reliability
- passive-aggressive behavior
- suppressing his feelings
- being motivated by love
- dry sense of humor
- leading by example

CHAPTER 2

Children with Mixed Temperaments

Some people are completely phlegmatic by temperament, or have only one or two characteristics of another temperament. Pure temperaments are easiest to identify and understand. Many more people have a mixed temperament, with phlegmatic being part of it. Due to the mix, it is more difficult to pinpoint their temperament or to predict how they might act in a particular circumstance. An almost infinite number of subtle differences exist between people.

In this chapter, I will discuss phlegmatic-sanguine and phlegmatic-melancholic mixes as they relate to parenting, teaching, and especially the spiritual life. If you have a child with a mixed temperament, keep these suggestions in mind as you read the rest of this book. I will be focusing on the pure phlegmatic temperament for the remainder of the book, since I could never enumerate all the possible variations.

People with mixed temperaments are often happier and more balanced than those with a pure temperament. They are more sympathetic to others' viewpoints, since they themselves do not always see things from one narrow perspective. Author Florence Littauer contends that people who have two horizontally connected temperaments on the temperament square are more balanced than those whose temperaments connect vertically.[6] In other words, a phlegmatic-melancholic, who has two introverted temperaments, will be more balanced than a phlegmatic-sanguine, who shares characteristics of both extroversion and introversion. Why would this be so? While both the phlegmatic and melancholic are introspective, the first values friendship and affirmation, while the second values ideals and right behavior. The phlegmatic-sanguine, on the other hand, is all about people, affection, and fitting in. It can be harder for a person of this mix to get things done and easier for him to ignore reason and act on emotion.

What about opposite temperaments? Many writers about the four temperaments, including Fr. Conrad Hock and Protestant author Tim LaHaye, believe that some people have a phlegmatic-choleric temperament. Art and Laraine Bennett argue that this is not possible and I agree with them.[7] If we recall that temperaments are based on reaction to stimuli, the near-impossibility of opposite combinations becomes clear. It's not just a matter of someone sometimes showing no emotion at all and other times getting violently angry. Rather, a phlegmatic-choleric combination would mean reacting slowly and mildly to stimuli and quickly forgetting in some situations, and reacting quickly and vehemently and hanging onto that reaction in other situations. Such varied reactions would not usually (if ever) exist in a healthy person.

Why then can a person seem to be both phlegmatic and choleric? First and most obviously, a person who thinks he is phlegmatic-choleric may not understand himself. Perhaps he is looking at his behavior only, and not getting to the roots of why he is reacting in a

---

[6] Florence Littauer, *Personality Plus for Couples: Understanding Yourself and the One You Love* (Grand Rapids, MI: F. H. Revell, 2001), 64.

[7] Art and Laraine Bennett, *The Temperament God Gave You: The Classic Key to Knowing Yourself, Getting along with Others, and Growing Closer to the Lord* (Manchester, NH: Sophia Institute Press, 2005), 199-200.

certain way. He may misunderstand where to draw the dividing line between various temperaments. Sometimes people modify their natural tendencies as they work on personal or spiritual growth. Or a child might learn to imitate the habits of his parents who have a different temperament than his. He may mask his true temperament to please others or to make his life easier.

Another problem arises from temperament tests. Many tests that rely on adjectives fail to define them. A reader's understanding of *stubborn,* for example, may not be the same as the test maker's. Other temperament tests rely on questions about how a person acts in specific situations. These actions may be influenced by not only temperament, but family upbringing, habit, culture, and peer pressure.

Extreme opposites sometimes look alike. A pure phlegmatic may be called stubborn because he digs in his heels when others try to force him to do something he does not want to. If others continue to push him, he might finally explode in rare anger. The choleric also responds negatively to most suggestions that were outside his agenda. He too might grow angry. But there is a difference.

The phlegmatic's anger comes only after he gently rebuffs attempts to make him do what he does not want to. At last he feels the need to protect his free will. He is angry that others are (in his view) trying to control him. Feeling devalued, he finally has a burst of temper. Since movement (physical or mental) is difficult for him, he almost always rejects a first suggestion to exert himself in a new direction. Given time to reflect, he gets used to the idea, sees its good points, and changes course. The choleric, on the other hand, resists suggestions from others because he needs to be in control of his life. He will likely argue at once. He too might come around, if he decides the activity will further one of his life goals.

If a phlegmatic is not aware of his inner motivations, he might mistakenly think he is acting like a choleric in such situations.

Sometimes a phlegmatic child will, through necessity, learn to act like a choleric. He might feel that he needs to scream in order to be noticed, so, since the affirmation he craves comes no other way, he screams. He not only adopts what he sees as the choleric's strengths, he also picks up the choleric's weaknesses.[8]

All of this can make it hard to pinpoint not only an adult's primary temperament, but also his secondary temperament, if any. On the other hand, as a parent working with your young child, you probably know his primary temperament quite well. You can recall what he was like in his first moments, and you have witnessed distinct patterns of behavior. Secondary temperaments can be a little harder to discern in young children. Most two-and three-year-olds throw temper tantrums, talk back, and test their parents, no matter what temperament they have. But by the school years, individual differences become clear.

Most phlegmatics will have a secondary temperament that is either sanguine or melancholic, although my experience is that 10 to 20 percent of people have a pure or nearly pure temperament. Here are some tips for working with your child who has a blended temperament. Remember, each child will have a slightly different blend, creating great variety. I will generalize for simplicity.

Phlegmatic-Sanguines

Phlegmatics and sanguines both love people. They both enjoy being part of the crowd. They are willing to overlook others' imperfections. They like everyone to get along. They tend to forget past hurts. They need affection, affirmation, and recreation. Neither is very neat or organized. All these factors make the phlegmatic-sanguine a bit lopsided in character compared to the phlegmatic-

---

[8] Littauer, 136.

melancholic. On the other hand, he is less introverted, more spontaneous, and more adventurous. He is quicker to forgive and forget faults and to move on, even from things he enjoys.

Everyone loves to have a phlegmatic-sanguine friend. Although quiet, he is also a bit mischievous. You might never suspect him of practical jokes until you see the twinkle in his eye. He is fun, he is kind, he is loyal. More thoughtful than a pure sanguine, more active than a pure phlegmatic, he is an asset to every party. He is less likely to be forgotten or overlooked than other phlegmatics. Friends, classmates, and co-workers all describe him as a "nice guy." He knows how to listen, but also how to enjoy himself. He is less serious than other phlegmatics.

The biggest challenge with this temperament is lack of self-discipline.

A child with this mix is not only hard to motivate, he is easily distracted from his task once he begins. He has a messy room and a disorganized desk. He puts off his assignments, then can't stay focused. He is often late for appointments.

He doesn't hesitate to lie to avoid conflict or to make someone else feel better. He avoids voicing hard truths. Details are not very important to him.

The phlegmatic-sanguine may also struggle with sins of the flesh, such as lust and gluttony. He is more in tune with beauty than most people. He can be attracted to people who are bad role models or mates. He is tempted by peer pressure, since he desires to fit in with the crowd. Relaxation, fun, and pleasure are high on his list of priorities. With the phlegmatic's sedentary lifestyle and the sanguine's appreciation for good food, he tends toward being overweight. He shows an over-all lack of forethought and discernment.

This child can lash out at siblings who try to control him, although his friends will consider him mild mannered. He might talk back—usually with the one-word answer *no*. This characteristic, combined with his stubbornness, makes it difficult for parents to pinpoint his temperament. He is not always the easy-going person you would expect a phlegmatic to be.

The phlegmatic-sanguine will probably be interested in the arts. Unfortunately, the arts are perennially pursued by people of low morals, especially low sexual morals. Participation could put your child in the face of the temptations he is least equipped to resist. A wise parent might steer his child away from performing arts such as drama to graphic arts or church choir.

Similarly, he needs guidance in choosing friends. He can easily fall under the influence of "charming" personalities who persuade him to join in immoral activities or take advantage of his reluctance to stand up for himself. He can fall prey to cults and predators. You cannot choose your child's friends, but you can choose the communities he is a part of, whether it be school, day care, sports, or youth group. Place him in a community in which the other children's parents have a strong faith and strong morals. Then let him drift towards those within the group he finds most attractive. Get to know his friends' parents. Invite the entire family over for dinner or movie nights. Host events at your home or volunteer to drive or chaperon.

Other adults might accuse you of being a "helicopter parent," always hovering around your child. But there is a balance between being too hands-off and being controlling. You do need to give your child the freedom to choose the good on his own. He must know that you have confidence in his decisions. Give him more freedom and responsibility gradually as he gets older, teaching him by word and example how to make prudent decisions. Tell him about the dangers he may face. Role play resisting temptation.

A father can teach his phlegmatic-sanguine daughter about the importance of modesty. He can teach her how to defend herself against boys and men who may not have her best interests at heart. He should get to know any boys who ask her out. As long as her father is affectionate and doesn't domineer her, she will appreciate his protection and guidance. He should tell her often how precious she is to him and that he expects others to treat her as well as she deserves.

The phlegmatic parent will find this child unexpectedly challenging. Learn to motivate him through love. Remember how you hate to be pushed. Give him plenty of time for quiet relaxation, but engage with him verbally when he wants to talk. Work together on being more organized and assertive.

The choleric parent may find this child pushes back—hard—when he feels controlled. Don't expect him to share your interests or your work ethic, but teach him how to do his chores consistently. Avoid harsh criticism of his shortcomings. Explore and learn to appreciate each others' differences.

Choleric and melancholic parents both should understand that this child *needs* plenty of time when he is not working. A phlegmatic-sanguine adult once told me that he left the Church because he never had any fun while he was living a good Christian life. Don't let this be your child. Books, movies, play dates, parties, and surprises are essential to his well-being. Avoid associating being Catholic with being serious or work-oriented. In many schools, his faith may by itself place him outside popular groups. Don't make it any harder for him. Introduce him to "cool" adults and young people who love the Lord. Get him involved in youth groups that combine faith and fun. Invite seminarians and young priests to dinner. Spend time just enjoying your relationship, with no other goals.

Phlegmatic-Melancholics

The phlegmatic-melancholic is a pure introvert. He takes time to reflect before making decisions, or even reacting to news. He needs plenty of rest, quiet, and time alone. He can be surprisingly goal-oriented for a phlegmatic, working hard to be the best in his chosen interests. He loves people, but sometimes wishes they would just go away and leave him alone. Unlike the pure phlegmatic, he hangs on to past hurts. Others find his facial expressions puzzling. They think he is angry or pouting when he is only daydreaming or reflecting.

Authors Art and Laraine Bennett write:

> When you are first entering a relationship with a phlegmatic-melancholic, you may be struck by how easy-going and agreeable they are, but be aware that they are not revealing the depth of their emotions to you. They are deeply sensitive and value harmony and high ideals within a relationship. As a result of his delayed and sometimes dull response, a phlegmatic-melancholic will be slower to speak out, tempted to procrastinate, and reticent.[9]

The phlegmatic-melancholic feels guilty for doing so little towards reaching the high goals he has for his life. He may be the proverbial physician who does not heal himself, knowledgeable and enthusiastic enough to advise others, but then watching them exceed him in execution.

He is the most loyal of all the temperaments or mixes.

He is also self-critical. He wishes he were sweeter like the pure phlegmatic. He makes plans for being more organized and diligent, but rarely follows through. He is afraid he will never have enough energy or perseverance to attain the greatness he longs for.

---

[9] Art and Lorraine Bennett, "The Phlegmatic/Melancholic," *Catholic Match,* http://www.catholicmatch.com/temperaments/phlegmatic/phlegmatic_melancholic.html (accessed November 12, 2015).

Experts say that this is the hardest temperament to understand. Others think him cold, while he has deep feelings which he longs to express. They think him strong and independent, while he is longing for friendship and a champion or buttress. They think him organized and task-oriented, while he struggles to order his life and needs love and affection. He waivers between trying to fit in with the group and disdaining trends and fashions. He can be painfully shy.

One of the great temptations of the phlegmatic-melancholic is towards passive-aggressive expressions of his emotions. He can also be very sensitive towards criticism. He takes criticism of his favorites books, movies, and interests personally and defends them with a surprising vehemence.

If he wants to, he can usually be a scholar, but he might not think it worth the effort. He loves family, tradition, and his small group of friends. He is sentimental. His strong principles compel him to speak up at times when he would rather not. He finds it necessary to sometimes hurt others' feelings and himself feels wretched for it.

Extroverted parents should take extra care to avoid harshness with the phlegmatic-melancholic. He will remember both unfair criticisms and encouraging words for decades. Point out where he has done right rather than where he has erred. Remind him of past successes. Show him you believe he can succeed.

This child functions best with plenty of sleep and quiet time. Don't expect him to be chipper in the morning. If he tells you he is tired, avoid giving him the third degree about it. Exhaustion does not necessarily mean he is ill or depressed. He will get exasperated if you try to tell him he shouldn't be tired. Just accept the fact and see that he gets rest.

Encourage him socially. He may need extra help with social skills, especially pointless chatting. Engage him in talk about his day or yours when he is refreshed from time alone. Gently coax him to give more than one-word answers to your questions and to reciprocate with questions for you. Once he begins talking about himself, he can fall into the opposite error of fixing the conversation on his interests and experiences, making others feel unappreciated. Teach him how to have real dialogs, rather than just taking turns with monologs. The more interaction he has with others, the more comfortable he will become. Recognize that he will always be more open and talkative one-on-one or in a small group of intimates than in a crowd.

CHAPTER 3

Two Famous Phlegmatics

What does a typical phlegmatic look like? Here are two phlegmatic saints, one male, one female. The Patriarch Abraham and Queen Esther both used their phlegmatic temperament for God's glory. Let's examine their lives from the perspective of temperament.

The Patriarch Abraham

The story of Abraham (called Abram at this point) begins with God calling him to travel to the Promised Land.

> Now the Lord said to Abram, "Go from your country and your kindred and your father's house to the land that I will show you. And I will make of you a great nation, and I will bless you, and make your name great, so that you will be a blessing...." So Abram went, as the Lord had told him; and Lot went with him. (Gn 12:1-2, 4)

In one way, this journey typifies the phlegmatic. He is compliant. He easily obeys. Yet here Abraham also acts against his natural temperament. He does not know what his ultimate destination will be.[10] The phlegmatic does not feel comfortable with an uncertain future. Change throws him off balance. He desires a clear, straight path that he can stay on for years. It seems that Abraham's path, the current he let lead him along, was doing the Lord's will. That was his life's focus. It made him one of the greatest men in history. The phlegmatic who truly puts God first can likewise change the world.

Next we see Abraham and his wife Sarah going to Egypt to escape famine. Abraham fears that Pharaoh will kill him to take his beautiful wife. So what does the Patriarch do? He tells people Sarah is his sister. This is technically true, but not the whole truth. Abraham is fearful. He fails to think through the problem, choosing the path that seems to save him from present suffering. He puts off planning how he will protect Sarah from an unlawful relationship. In the end, God, not Abraham, intervenes to help her. The phlegmatic looks for present peace. He hopes that the future will take care of itself. He sometimes puts off acting until it is too late. Fear and indecision can paralyze him.

After some time, Abraham settles near Bethel and becomes a rich man. But he and his nephew Lot both have so many men and flocks that their servants start quarreling. As a phlegmatic, Abraham hates conflict. He tells Lot to choose where he wants to settle. He is indifferent to the choice. All he wants is peace! Even the status quo can be set aside if it saves him from conflict. If necessary, Abraham will move his household elsewhere. But Lot chooses Sodom, so Abraham is able to stay put.

God promises that Abraham with be the father of a multitude. When Sarah does not conceive, she offers Abraham her slave girl Hagar as a concubine. Abraham agrees without argument. He is will-

---

[10] See Heb 11:8.

ing to have a child with Hagar to fulfill God's promise. Later, he at Sarah's instigation sends Hagar and her son Ishmael away. The Bible tells us that he is "very distressed" at this request, but it does not tell us that he argues or insists on keeping his son in the family.[11] Perhaps he is afraid to speak up for what he thinks is right. This is a common phlegmatic failing. When God assures him that he will take care of Ishmael, Abraham does as Sarah demands.

Twice, Abraham lets his strong family ties overcome his fears. Both relate to Lot. First, he rescues Lot when he is taken captive during a war. Then he pleads with the Lord to spare Sodom if he finds even ten righteous people there—obviously hoping that Lot and his family will make up the bulk of those ten. The phlegmatic loves his family without making a fuss about it. He can be fiercely loyal. Abraham's argument for God to spare Sodom is done respectfully, in small steps. It is almost as if he is afraid of his request overwhelming God! He is apologetic, yet persevering. When a phlegmatic makes up his mind, few people can budge him.

Then comes the climax of Abraham's story. God asks him to sacrifice Isaac, who is the promised, miraculous heir. Abraham does not hesitate.

> Then Abraham said to his young men, "Stay here with the donkey; the boy and I will go over there; we will worship, and then we will come back to you." Abraham took the wood of the burnt offering and laid it on his son Isaac, and he himself carried the fire and the knife. So the two of them walked on together. Isaac said to his father Abraham, "Father!" And he said, "Here I am, my son." He said, "The fire and the wood are here, but where is the lamb for a burnt offering?" Abraham said, "God himself will provide the lamb for a burnt offering, my son." So the two of them walked on together. (Gn 22:5-8)

---

[11] See Gn 21:8-12.

Twice in this passage, Abraham indicates that he expects Isaac to live. First, he tells the servants to wait for the two of them to return. Then he tells Isaac that God will provide the lamb for the sacrifice. (This statement is one of the greatest prophecies of all time. God fulfills Abraham's words by sending a ram, yes, but also by providing his own Son as the sacrificial Lamb of God.) The New Testament tells us that Abraham has such faith in God, he believes that even if Isaac dies, God will resurrect him.[12] His temperament bolsters his trust.

The peace-loving phlegmatic hopes, sometimes unreasonably, that problems will work themselves out. Abraham's hope is not so unreasonable, since he has God's promise of countless descendants through Isaac. Besides, God has set a precedent. When Ishmael needed help, God came to his aid, saving him from dying of thirst after Abraham sent him and Hagar into the desert. God's mercy has spared one of Abraham's sons already. Why not the other? This highlights one of the most overlooked characteristics of the phlegmatic. When making hard decisions, he longs for others to stand firmly with him. The more they support and protect him, the more confident he will be with his next decision. He knows he is not alone. His earlier success energizes him. So Abraham was energized by God's faithfulness and received the confidence in God and himself that led him to believe in the impossible.

Abraham, the phlegmatic that was once too frightened to acknowledge that Sarah was his wife, through the grace of God has the courage to offer up his only son. He shows us both the bad and the good in the phlegmatic temperament.

---

[12] See Heb 11:18-19.

Queen Esther

Phlegmatic women tend to be supporters of leaders of other temperaments. They express their temperament quietly, often at home. Few become famous. Esther would probably never have been known to history, except for the special circumstances she found herself in. She shows how one phlegmatic person can make a huge impact for God by following his will.

Esther's story is found in the biblical book named after her. King Ahaserus (also known as Xerxes) is married to a beautiful woman named Vashti. When the king holds a banquet, he calls his wife to come show off her beauty to his guests. The choleric Vashti refuses. Ahaserus responds by deposing the queen and seeking another wife. He eventually chooses Esther, a Jewish girl who is Vashti's temperamental opposite.

Esther spends a year in the king's harem, being prepared to meet him. When at last it is time for her to do so, she does exactly as the eunuch in charge of the harem advises her. Throughout the story, we see Esther's compliance and obedience, two typically phlegmatic traits. Perhaps these are what attract Ahaserus to her so that he makes her his queen.

Mordecai is Esther's cousin. He raised her after her parents died. On his advice, Esther keeps her Jewish heritage secret. She shows her loyalty to her cousin, even though he is no longer in authority over her. The phlegmatic, as a lover of the status quo, has the most loyal temperament. She (in this case) listens to those she loves. She rouses herself to do heroic deeds for them. Her calm exterior hides deep feelings. Family, tribe, and nation have her allegiance.

Haman is the king's chief adviser. He is ambitious, envious, and vengeful. He makes the people of Susa bow down in reverence to him. But Mordecai sees this bowing as a kind of idolatry. He refuses to bow before anyone but God. When Haman discovers Mordecai is Jewish, he plots revenge on the entire Jewish people.

The phlegmatic can also be very discreet when necessary. She has the classic poker face. No one can guess what she is thinking or feeling, or if anything at all is going on behind her mask of a face. God uses this characteristic to surprise Haman, who has no idea that the queen is related to Mordecai. Esther does not reveal anything about her heritage or her concern for her people. She gives Haman no chance to form a response to her accusations against him.

But at first, Esther does not know of Haman's plot. She learns of it when some of her servants tell her that Mordecai is distressed. Mordecai asks her to plead for the Jewish people before Ahaserus. Esther replies:

> All the king's servants and the people of the king's provinces know that if any man or woman goes to the king inside the inner court without being called, there is but one law; all alike are to be put to death, except the one to whom the king holds out the golden scepter that he may live. And I have not been called to come in to the king these thirty days. (Est 4:11)

The phlegmatic resists being told how to act. With family and close friends, she may initially respond with protests or excuses. But given some time, she usually comes around. Esther wants to do what is right, but she is fearful. She is not used to speaking out, especially against the rules. She likes to keep the peace, not make waves, do as she is told. Here the two authorities over her—the old (Mordecai) and the new (Ahaserus)—oblige her to act in opposite ways. How can she decide which to follow?

The phlegmatic often finds herself paralyzed by indecision, when two opposing choices both seem reasonable, or when two people she loves have opposite expectations. The last queen was deposed for simply defying her husband. Can Esther dare break the law that is punishable by death? She owes loyalty to Ahaserus as both her husband and her king. But she owes loyalty to Mordecai as the man who brought her up, and to her people. Mordecai reminds her that her own safety is not guaranteed either. "And who knows whether you have not come to the kingdom for such a time as this?[13]" She recognizes that her highest allegiance is to God. His will reigns over all. She finally resigns herself, probably with a sigh, then utters her famous words, "If I perish, I perish."[14]

Esther still needs others' support to carry out her task. She asks the Jews in Susa to fast three days before she approaches the king. The phlegmatic needs to know that she is not alone, that others support her. She relies on their steadfastness to buttress her strength.

Even still, Esther approaches Ahaserus in a phlegmatic manner. She enters his court quietly, waiting for him to notice her, unsure of her fate. When he extends his scepter in mercy and asks what she wants, she does not immediately speak of Haman's plot. She puts off the final confrontation, inviting the king and Haman to a banquet. Few things freeze the phlegmatic as much as the need to publicly confront someone. She will endure almost any hardship rather than speak a difficult truth. At the banquet, Esther again puts off speaking, inviting them to a second feast. Then at last she knows she must speak or lose the courage to do it at all. She does not accuse Haman straight out, but appeals to the king's love for her, telling him her life is in danger. When Ahaserus' anger is aroused against the enemy, she has the courage to name him.

Esther shows how even an indecisive, timid phlegmatic can change history by relying on the grace of God. With others' prayer, affirmation, and moral support, the phlegmatic temperament brings great glory to God.

---

[13] Verse 15.
[14] Verse 17.

CHAPTER 4

The Meaning and Means of Spiritual Growth

What is *spiritual growth?* How can people grow spiritually? What is the goal of the spiritual life? Before trying to help your child grow spiritually, you should know the answers to these questions.

The Fathers of the Second Vatican Council wrote:

> All Christians in any state or walk of life are called to the fullness of Christian life and to the perfection of charity.[15]

Notice it says "all Christians," and "the fullness of Christian life." Your child is not called to be a mediocre Christian. He is not called to climb half way up the mountain to God. He is called to "the *perfection* of Christian charity." In other words, God wants your child to become a saint. He is called to love God with his whole heart, mind, soul, and strength, and his neighbor as himself.[16]

Your child has his own will. As a phlegmatic, he has a "hidden will of iron."[17] You cannot force him to do anything. You can make

---

[15] *Lumen Gentium,* no. 40 § 2, quoted in CCC, no. 2013.
[16] See Mt 22:37-40.
[17] Littauer, 209.

many spiritual growth plans for him, but you cannot make him act on them. He must choose to work with God's grace to become holy. My hope is that this book will help you increase the likelihood that he will long for holiness and work hard for it. In forming your child's mind and heart, you must respect his God-given freedom. Working with his temperament should help you in the endeavor.

Formation of Conscience

Conversion is a life-long process. There is always room for more knowledge, more conforming of the will to God. There is always room for love to be more perfect. You are helping your child start on the road to God. He must see it through to the end.

As you teach him right from wrong, how to love God and others, you help him to form his conscience. A well-formed conscience enables him to choose good and reject evil. It helps him overcome temptation throughout his life.

As he receives the intellectual formation of knowing what is right, your child also needs to form habits of virtuous behavior. The habits of childhood can last a lifetime. When these habits are reinforced by the virtuous examples of others, they provide the foundation for a rich spiritual life.

The Catechism of the Catholic Church says:

> It is important for every person to be sufficiently present to himself in order to hear and follow the voice of his conscience. This requirement of *interiority* is all the more necessary as life often distracts us from any reflection, self-examination, or introspection.[18]

---

18 CCC, no. 1779.

Reflection and introspection come naturally for the phlegmatic. This is his advantage over extroverts.

The Catechism continues:

> The education of the conscience is a lifelong task. From the earliest years, it awakens the child to the knowledge and practice of the interior law recognized by conscience. Prudent education teaches virtue; it prevents or cures fear, selfishness and pride, resentment arising from guilt, and feelings of complacency, born of human weakness and faults. The education of the conscience guarantees freedom and engenders peace of heart.[19]

Isn't that what we all want for our children?

Growing in Intimacy with Christ

Christian perfection is not just a matter of moral righteousness. It is a matter of love. The goal of the spiritual life is an intimate relationship with God through Jesus Christ. Your child will grow in virtue not just through his human effort, but by cooperating with God's grace. Grace comes to us when we obey God's will, when we spend time in prayer, and especially through the sacraments.

> A virtue is an [sic.] habitual and firm disposition to do the good. It allows the person not only to perform good acts, but to give the best of himself. The virtuous person tends toward the good with all his sensory and spiritual powers; he pursues the good and chooses it in concrete action.[20]

You can measure your child's spiritual growth, to a certain extent, by his effort to overcome his faults, his desire to pray and the care he takes in praying, and his love for the Mass and the Sacrament of Reconciliation. At the same time, spiritual growth, since it is

---

[19] CCC, no. 1784.
[20] CCC, no. 1803.

growth in intimacy with Christ, is a secret, mysterious process. Only God can discern how much your child is taking the faith to heart, rather than just conforming outwardly to the behavior he believes you want to see.

His psychological maturity will have a great impact on his relationship with God. The more he matures as a person, the deeper his love relationship with Christ can become. We cannot expect him to love God at a level that is beyond the capacity of his years. Children are self-centered. As long as your child sees you and your spouse primarily through the lens of his needs, he will see God the same way. He will see God as someone who supplies for his needs and wants. This is normal and healthy.

In adolescence, he will begin to look at God more analytically. He will ask questions and desire answers. He will enjoy finding logical reasons for the faith. He will try to understand God's character at a deeper level.[21] As part of growing up, he will go through a period of questioning what you have taught him. Try to see this period as an opportunity for great spiritual growth in your child, rather than something for you to fear. Your prayers and sacrifices for your child, as well as your love, understanding, and example, can help him make the faith his own.

Steps in Spiritual Change

Before you can motivate your child to change, you should understand how people are motivated. Each temperament requires a slightly different motivation technique, yet everyone shares some basic similarities. Over the years, I have come to recognize several

---

[21] Fr. Benedict Groeschel provides an excellent explanation of these stages in his book *Spiritual Passages: The Psychology of Spiritual Development.*

steps that I go through before I make a major change in my spiritual life.

1. Someone else's idea

When helping your phlegmatic child to change, you must first tell him what the goal is. Show him it is important by practicing it yourself. If you want to teach him a strong work ethic, you must cultivate one yourself. If you want to teach him empathy, show concern when he is disappointed. This instruction and modeling only comprises the first step towards his making a change.

2. Conviction that a change is necessary

The movement from a vague awareness that others think you should change, to conviction that you must, often results from a crisis. For example, a boy who never listened to his mother when she said he needed to learn to swim might be suddenly motivated after he nearly drowns. He realizes she was right!

Art and Laraine Bennett describe this step as being able to change. They say a person must believe he can succeed before he will make a commitment.[22] When trying to form your phlegmatic child's character, give him lots of encouragement, share examples of others who have succeeded, and remind him of past successes.

3. The will to change

Once a person is convinced of the need for change, he must choose it. At first he chooses the over all goal of change. Then he must choose to follow through when temptations or distractions plague him.

---

[22] Bennetts, 169.

Other people can help with the first two steps. With the third a person is on his own—except, of course, for grace. Only you can make the choice to change your life. Only your child can make the choice to change his. But you can help him strengthen his will, making it more likely he will choose the change you are proposing.

Prayer is at the root of all true spiritual change, because prayer brings your child into God's presence. In prayer (whether the liturgy of the Church or personal prayer), he meets God. He learns about God's goodness. His heart is moved to follow God's will. God gives him the grace to say *yes*. This is particularly true of meditation on Sacred Scripture. It informs your child's mind, moves his will, and opens his heart to grace. Begin working with your child to learn how to practice mental prayer as early as possible. Later in this book I give you several helps to do this.

Also for this step, motivate your child with stories of admirable people who made the right choices. Use the lives of phlegmatic saints and heroes as examples. These stories will touch his heart. An older child can write *what-if* stories: What if Abraham had been too afraid to set out from Ur? What if Esther had not risked her life to beg for the lives of her people? Use fables and morality tales such as those in *The Book of Virtues* or books from the list in chapter 13 for this purpose. Adapt this exercise for elementary school children by discussing the stories orally.

See chapter 6, Motivating Your Phlegmatic Child, for more on this step.

4. Specific goals

Once your child has decided to change, he needs to choose concrete goals to make that change. Help him start small. The phlegmatic will be overwhelmed if you give him too much information or too many steps at once. Let him succeed one step at a time.

Be patient. Real change does not happen overnight. The start of the road has the roughest terrain. "At the proper time, you will reap a harvest, if you do not give up."[23]

---

[23] Gal 6:9.

CHAPTER 5

Modeling God's Fatherhood

N ow that we have a basic understanding of the phlegmatic and the meaning of spiritual growth, let's examine how the family can provide the love and support he needs to survive. The family is a domestic church, the Church in miniature.

> The Christian home is the place where children receive the first proclamation of the faith. For this reason the family home is rightly called "the domestic church," a community of grace and prayer, a school of human virtues and of Christian charity. [24]

God designed the domestic church to begin forming children in love of God and neighbor. In your family, you and your spouse stand in the place of God for your children. You give them their first glimpse of God's fatherhood and his loving care for his children. You teach them the importance of obedience to authority, especially divine authority. Likewise, siblings teach each other how to love their neighbors as themselves. As a whole family, you instill the idea that the spiritual life is not meant to be lived in isolation. It is not just a matter of "me and God," but of being a member of God's family.

---

[24] CCC, no. 1666.

Modeling Spiritual Growth

When I first began blogging at Contemplative Homeschool, I intended to share my prayer-focused homeschooling method with the world. I quickly realized that parents could not teach their children about prayer if they were not prayerful themselves. My aim shifted to teaching adults how to grow in their faith so that they could pass this knowledge on to their children.

One of the most powerful ways of modifying your child's behavior is modeling—that is, practicing—the behavior you want to see in him. As author Mary Sheedy Kurcinka says, pre-teens want to be like their parents.[25] Your young children will try to copy you.

Modeling is more important for your child's spiritual life than in any other area. Think about it. Teaching the faith goes beyond teaching the facts and dates of history, which may seldom impact your child's life. Being Catholic is not just for the classroom. It impacts every moment of our lives.

For too long parents have let Catholic school teachers or religious education instructors take all the responsibility for teaching kids the faith. "Religion" has been just another class to take, having little more significance for kids' lives than their science projects do. No wonder so many youth disengage from the faith after Confirmation! They feel like they have graduated from religious education. They "know" everything they need to for making an adult commitment to the faith. Done.

The Christian faith is not just an academic subject, and you don't want your children to think of it as one. Although it's vitally important to know about the faith, knowledge is just the beginning. The Catechism tells us we were made to know, love, and serve God.

---

[25] Mary Sheedy Kurcinka, *Kids, Parents, and Power Struggles* (New York: Harper Collins, 2000), 58.

Notice, it doesn't say *know the faith*, but *know God*. We learn the faith in order to have an intimate relationship with God through Jesus Christ. The Church teaches us how. Then we must practice it.

Even school subjects must be practiced to be learned. What if you taught your child physical education by reading a book about sports? Would he ever become an athlete? Would he even truly understand how to play the games? Or what if you taught art by lecturing about color theory, but never opened a box a crayons? Not much chance of rearing an artist that way, is there? Nor is there much chance of raising a saint if the faith remains something to study, rather than to live.

Pope St. John Paul II wrote:

> For Christian parents the mission to educate, a mission rooted, as we have said, in their participation in God's creating activity, has a new specific source in the sacrament of marriage, which consecrates them for the strictly Christian education of their children: that is to say, it calls upon them to share in the very authority and love of God the Father and Christ the Shepherd, and in the motherly love of the Church, and it enriches them with wisdom, counsel, fortitude and all the other gifts of the Holy Spirit in order to help the children in their growth as human beings and as Christians.[26]

Jesus said, "Let the little children come to me, and do not hinder them."[27] Your child is naturally (and supernaturally since Baptism) designed to seek God. If his hunger for spiritual things is not satisfied in the Church, he will look for satisfaction elsewhere. Not hindering him does not just mean moving out of his way. It means showing him the way. It means bringing him to Jesus. This is your God-given responsibility, no matter how your children learn their

---

[26] *Familiaris Consortio,* no. 38.
[27] Mt 19:4.

academic subjects or if they attend religious education classes. You are your child's first—and most important—teacher of the faith.

Catholic school teachers or religious educators can't give your child everything he needs to become intimate with Christ, because they don't live with your child. They are not well situated to show him how to behave when his plans fall through, when he is sick, or angry, or in a crisis. *But you are.*

Now, you may be discouraged, thinking, *But I'm so imperfect! I sin all the time.* Well, of course. You are a fallen human. God knows this better than you do. He has provided for it. You can use your weaknesses to your child's advantage.

You have the opportunity to demonstrate to your child that Original Sin exists. Yes, everyone in your family—and in the human race—is fallen. You are all tempted. You all sin. You also have the opportunity to demonstrate God's mercy and grace. When you sin against a family member, acknowledge it. Don't neglect to tell your child you are sorry when you discipline him too harshly or yell instead of teach. Forgive him when he sins against you or other family members. Don't hold a grudge. Don't prejudge him. Go to confession often, and take him with you once he reaches the age of reason. End every night by hugging him and saying, *I love you*—no matter how old he is, no matter what he has done.

Again, parents of different temperaments will find different aspects of this challenging, but it's too important for your family's well-being for you to shrug off your responsibility. If you want to help your child curb the negative aspects of his temperament, begin by curbing yours.

If your spouse is better at being open and vulnerable than you, consider letting him be the primary teacher about temperaments and spiritual growth.

Pray every day. Pray morning prayer with your kids at home-school or on the weekends. Pray before every meal, even in public. Teach your child to make the Sign of the Cross slowly and reverent-ly. Don't rush through the words, and don't allow him to do so ei-ther. Pray the Rosary with the whole family, at least now and then. Pray briefly as a family before bed. Set aside a specific time and place daily to pray mental prayer, talking to God from the heart, for a minimum of fifteen minutes. Make it your top priority. Be willing to give up everything before missing your intimate time alone with the Lord, and make sure your child knows about it.

Attend Mass every Sunday and Holy Day of Obligation. If you homeschool, try to work some extra Mass times into your schedule. Don't overwhelm yourself by thinking you need to go every day if you have an infant or toddler. Just do what you can. My youngest is four. Two years ago, we started attending Mass with other home-schoolers one Friday a month, with breakfast at McDonald's after-ward. This year we are trying to attend an extra Mass weekly.

Be active in your parish or diocese as your family life permits. Do you have a gift you can share? Can you sing in the choir, lector, or help with funeral lunches? If you have little ones and can't take on a new commitment, could you donate flowers from your garden to decorate the sanctuary or be a member of the prayer chain? You could also volunteer at a local crisis pregnancy center, or donate to the food bank regularly.

Talk about the faith as a family. On Sunday evenings, discuss the Mass readings and homily around the dinner table, beginning with the youngest family member who can talk. Our preschooler's usual contribution is recalling what color vestments the priest wore. Dis-cuss current events in light of the faith.

Treat your spouse with love and respect. Never criticize him publicly, and absolutely never criticize him to your children. Make your spouse second only to God in your life. Show your child what a Christian marriage should look like.

If all this sounds like a lot, remember that you don't have to be perfect to be a good role model. You just have to be striving to grow closer to Christ. Your willingness to be vulnerable, to admit your mistakes, can be as valuable to your child as the elusive moral perfection.

Parental Temperaments

Every Christian can benefit from having a spiritual director. The phlegmatic adult, even if he plans to seek one out, may never follow through. In his childhood years, you are his spiritual director. Your role is all the more important, since you may be the only director he ever has. The hope is, however, that once he has formed the habit of taking direction from you, he will easily gravitate towards seeking direction in adulthood.

If your direction is going to benefit your child, he must know that you care about him and appreciate his gifts. It is easy for parents to overlook the phlegmatic while they concentrate on their "more difficult" children. Parents of various temperaments will each have different issues.

The sanguine parent resembles the phlegmatic in loving people and being disorganized and messy. The sanguine, however, may not understand his child's need for quiet and time alone. The sanguine's constant chatter can wear the phlegmatic out. A parent who breaks the rules may embarrass or worry his child.[28] The parent's lack of discipline will not help the phlegmatic to learn responsibility or to reach his potential. The sanguine parent must take care that an over-

---

[28] Florence Littauer, *Personality Plus for Parents: Understanding What Makes Your Child Tick* (Grand Rapids, MI: F. H. Revell, 2000), 142-144.

emphasis on fun doesn't discourage his child from growing up, a real danger for this temperament. Give your child time to adapt, instead of expecting him to run from one activity or idea to the next. Recognize that although he likes to have fun, he does not feel comfortable breaking rules, however trivial they may seem to you. Don't expect him to be exuberant. A quiet contentment means he is enjoying the moment. Never force him to express his feelings more openly. Instead, smile at him and allow him to respond.

The phlegmatic parent will understand and appreciate his phlegmatic child. Such a father and son will enjoy fishing trips together, sitting near each other for hours, neither saying a word. A phlegmatic mother and daughter might share a girls' movie night or read the same books and discuss them. On the other hand, the parent may be tempted to let the child do all the things he or she could not do in childhood—lie late in bed, spend lots of time watching TV or on the computer, and put off homework and housework. This parent must also be careful of making the child's environment unrealistically conflict-free, so that he is unable to face conflict as an adult.

The melancholic parent shares the phlegmatic child's need for quiet and solitude. However, he might not understand his child's need for relaxation and entertainment. The melancholic parent should be careful not to expect adult behavior from one so young. He should look to his own failings and shortcomings so that he is not too hard on the child. He should strive to compliment the good he sees, remembering that the best motivators for the phlegmatic are affection and encouragement. Physical affection may not be natural to this parent, and the phlegmatic child may not express a need or desire for it. But a squeeze, a hug, or a pat at the right time can convey the sympathy and encouragement your child needs.

The choleric parent will find it the hardest to understand his phlegmatic child. Frustrated by his child's "stubbornness" and lack of motivation, he will be tempted to do everything for his child, just to make sure it gets done.[29] The choleric never shrinks from a challenge. He must recognize that his child hates conflict. He must pick his battles, deciding what is really worth upsetting his child over. A phlegmatic who is pushed to do too much may begin to resist everything.[30] Likewise, harsh criticism can cause the phlegmatic to act out in a passive-aggressive manner. The choleric parent needs to learn to value his phlegmatic child for his character, rather than any accomplishments he may have. Recognize that your child is very different from you, not only in action, but in what he considers important and how he views the world. The two can help each other be more balanced, if they understand each other and are willing to work together.

The Importance of Fathers

Fathers, especially since they tend to be the primary breadwinners, play an important role in teaching their kids a strong work ethic. Fathers who emphasize work to the detriment of faith or family will only deepen their phlegmatic child's distaste for work. A good life-work balance, on the other hand, teaches him that he can still have time for hobbies and relaxation while being a responsible worker. If his father never takes time for fun, he can come to view work and relaxation as incompatible. Experts suggest that fathers have a slogan such as "fun after the work is done." This shows your child that relaxation should not be used as an escape from duty, but a natural consequence of completing one's work. Then the pleasure he experi-

---

29 Ibid., 150.
30 Littauer, *Parents,* 153.

ences in relaxing reinforces and strengthens the satisfaction of a job well done.[31]

A phlegmatic girl may dream of a knight coming to protect and save her.[32] Her father can be that knight, shielding her from the harshness of the world, encouraging her, showing her affection, backing her up when others oppose her, and being on her side, rather than taking an adversarial stance towards her. Similarly, a phlegmatic boy may worship heroes. His father can guide him to choose the right heroes, protecting him from those who would take advantage of his naiveté and distaste for saying no.[33] You can become your son's hero and role model by being understanding and gentle and listening to his concerns.

Heritage Foundation Senior Fellow Dr. Patrick Fagan has said to fathers, "To the extent that your son experiences you, the great, strong giant in his life, as somebody who delights in his presence, he grows in confidence in himself. To the extent that he experiences you as distant, he lacks confidence in himself." Fagan notes that daughters also need this experience, which must begin in the toddler years.[34] Such a relationship with one's father is crucial for the often-timid phlegmatic.

A father who protects and supports his wife will also give his phlegmatic child a sense of security. A man willing to be his wife's champion makes his child believe he will be his champion too. The child will love and respect both parents.

---

[31] "10 Ways to Teach Your Children a Great Work Ethic," *All ProDad,* http://www.allprodad.com/10-ways-to-teach-your-children-a-great-work-ethic/ (accessed December 31, 2015).

[32] Littauer, *Parents,* 133.

[33] Ibid.

[34] Tom McDonough, "Great Dads Foster Self-Confidence in Children," *Catholic Herald,* http://catholicherald.com/stories/Great-Dads-Foster-Self-Confidence-in-Children,4285. Jan. 10, 2001.

Studies show that girls tend to relate to potential spouses similarly to the way they related to their fathers. Since men in general tend to talk less than women, a father can be excellent company for the child who desires quiet companionship more than heart-felt conversations. If her father accepts and supports her, she will more likely have the self-confidence to look for a supportive mate. She will also feel more comfortable with herself and her role in the world.

Gentleness is key. The phlegmatic child may fear a gruff or outspoken father. A choleric father should take extra care here. If he is the main disciplinarian but does not spend much time getting to know the child, the phlegmatic will shrink from him. This will adversely affect the child's relationship with God as well.

Once our boys hit age nine or ten, they take turns going for walks with my husband. They discuss anything that is on their mind, but especially private struggles, or issues their brothers may be too young to handle. If someone learns a new word he is afraid is inappropriate, or sees a headline about an adult subject, I tell him to ask Dad about it on their next walk. If I had any daughters, I would take a similar role with them. The phlegmatic child may particularly enjoy this one-on-one time with Dad. He does not have to vie with siblings for attention. He feels valued and affirmed. He may even take the opportunity to share his deep feelings or struggles if you do not push him to do so.

Pope St. John Paul II wrote about the role of fathers:

> In revealing and in reliving on earth the very fatherhood of God, a man is called upon to ensure the harmonious and united development of all the members of the family: he will perform this task by exercising generous responsibility for the life conceived under the heart of the mother, by a more solicitous commitment to education, a task he shares with his wife, by work which is never a cause of division in the family but promotes its unity and stability, and by means of the witness he gives of an adult Christian life

which effectively introduces the children into the living experience of Christ and the Church.[35]

---

[35] *Familiaris Consortio*, no. 25.

CHAPTER 6

Motivating Your Phlegmatic Child

Reading books and articles about the temperaments has had one major frustration for me. Many authors and theorists, including Fr. Conrad Hock, are dismissive of the phlegmatic. In his work *The Four Temperaments and the Spiritual Life*, Fr. Hock averages 3,000 words about each of the other three temperaments, but writes less than 300 about the phlegmatic. These sentences make up the entire section "The Training of Phlegmatic Children":

> The training of phlegmatic children is very difficult, because external influence has little effect upon them and internal personal motives are lacking. It is necessary to explain everything most minutely to them, and repeat it again and again, so that at least some impression may be made to last, and to accustom them by patience and charity to follow strictly a well-planned rule of life. The application of corporal punishment is less dangerous in the education of phlegmatic children; it is much more beneficial to them than to other children, especially to those of choleric or melancholic temperament.[36]

---

[36] Hock, 5:5.

Not only are these words discouraging for parents, some of this advice is dead wrong. Nagging will cause a phlegmatic child to push back by moving even more slowly. Repeating minute details will only wear him out. Corporal punishment may make him feel controlled and demoralized.

Then how does one motivate the phlegmatic? How can parents help this child reach his potential—or at least keep his room clean? The question of motivation may be parents' primary concern. Let's first look at the larger question of the phlegmatic's root sin.

Root Sin of Sloth

Every person has a root sin (or two) that presents his biggest barrier to holiness. This root sin is usually related to his temperament. The phlegmatic's root sin is sloth. He is typically viewed as lazy, but he can work very hard once he is motivated. The key is to get the phlegmatic started in the right direction. Once he has started—unless he also has sanguine tendencies—he will keep going without needing to be pushed or persuaded. But this assumes that he was interiorly motivated to begin with. If you tell your phlegmatic child to clean his room, for example, he may start half-heartedly and fall into idleness as soon as you walk away. What if you suggest he paint a picture to overcome his boredom? In this case, he might protest at first, but half an hour later he has persuaded himself that he likes the idea. He gets out his paints and spends hours on his project, reluctant to stop for meals or bedtime.

I like to think of the phlegmatic as a still pool. He wants to remain perfectly calm. Any ripples disturb his inner peace. Those ripples can be conflicts, disagreements, change, physical activity, or interruptions. He will avoid these disturbances by hiding, clamming up, or digging in his heels. Passive-aggressive behavior constantly tempts him.

Another way of looking at the phlegmatic is as the embodiment of inertia. We can substitute *phlegmatic* for *object* in Sir Isaac Newton's first law of physics: A phlegmatic in motion tends to stay in motion and a phlegmatic at rest tends to stay at rest. This explains why the phlegmatic can astonish others by his persistent hard work in a few key areas. Many authors believe that the monks who painstakingly copied and decorated medieval manuscripts were phlegmatics. When animated, the phlegmatic can be patient and attentive to detail. What bores others doesn't bother him. The phlegmatic is the consummate conservative. He will keep to his course, come what may. It is easier for him to keep going than to stop. Stopping implies change, ripples in the pool.

What we want to do is help the phlegmatic child motivate himself, rather than try to push him from outside. This takes patience, gentleness, and encouragement.

Chores for Phlegmatics

Phlegmatics can be the most pleasant people to spend time with until there is work to be done. Your phlegmatic child has good intentions, but often little motivation or follow-through. One way to get around having to nag him is to work with him. Especially if there is a big job to do, you will expend less time and energy digging in and working alongside your child than monitoring him.

Phlegmatics get overwhelmed easily. Even thinking about how much there is to do can depress the phlegmatic. Break down large tasks into smaller chunks to be tackled one by one with breaks in between.

Another way to minimize discipline problems is to give your child a task you can easily monitor, or one that is more suited to his talents and interests.

Here are some chores that a phlegmatic may do without much resistance:

- Set the table.
- Clear the table.
- Load or unload the dishwasher.
- Watch younger siblings.
- Cook or bake.
- Pick vegetables or flowers.
- Help with grocery shopping.
- Research products, nutrition, recipes, books and movies, etc.
- Put laundry in the washer or dryer.
- Design a garden.
- Clean the outside of kitchen appliances.
- Organize small spaces (such as one drawer of a desk).
- Walk the dog.

He can easily forget even routine tasks if not reminded. This is why an organizational scheme is so helpful to him. Chore charts work well, but don't assign him to do too much record-keeping himself. It is probably best—at least until the teen years—for you to make his lists and simply let him check the items off. He won't easily stick to the record-keeping without your reminders. If you are giving him new tasks to do, I suggest waiting to use the chart until he has started to make the tasks a habit. Otherwise completing the chart can itself seem like another task he has to do and overwhelm him.

One practical way to motivate him is to show him his options. If a teenaged phlegmatic is reluctant to get a part-time job, for instance, suggest some that may interest him. He may be paralyzed by indecision, overwhelmed by the amount of mental energy he must put into the task.

Reminders of past successes also help, especially when a large or new task is before him. The realization that he has succeeded in something this hard or harder before empowers him.

The phlegmatic is more interested in beauty than in order. Using this attraction to beauty, you can motivate him. In school this may mean encouraging artistic talent, teaching calligraphy (or just good, old-fashioned cursive), and doing picture studies and nature study. Setting the table correctly is a good job for the phlegmatic that combines beauty with order. Let doing it well become second nature to him. Allow him to make centerpieces, do artistic napkin folding, or use the special china now and then for fun.

A simpler life with fewer toys or outfits might also help to keep the mess under control. You could reward hard work with a trip to a museum, a new box of crayons, or a book by a favorite author.

Protecting Him from Being Overwhelmed

When the phlegmatic is overwhelmed, he is literally almost unable to listen to new directives or suggestions. He will tune you out. He may completely detach emotionally from the situation, doing what he must, but under silent protest.[37]

He needs lots of down-time in order to function at his best. Some people say that only sleep rejuvenates him,[38] but this is untrue. Vegging in front of the TV or reading a book can also help him recharge. However, depending on how much work he has done, recharging may take hours or days. If one day he has worked really

---

[37] Littauer, *Couples,* 197.
[38] "Phlegmatic (Introvert)," *The Five Basic Temperaments,* http://fivetemperaments.weebly.com/phlegmatic.html (accessed December 31, 2015).

hard with few breaks, the next day he may find himself completely unmotivated, even for tasks he normally enjoys. He seems unable to bring himself to do anything, even if he is not physically exhausted. Therefore, it does not make sense to push him to do too much at once, especially on major projects. In the long run, he will probably not finish earlier and may even take longer than if he were left to choose his own pace. It's important to understand that this reaction is not just laziness. It is not so much a willed decision to pamper himself after working hard (although the phlegmatic does like to do that too), as a draining of the psychological energy he needs to continue moving.

Ample time to relax helps him transition from one activity to the next. After school, for example, you can give him half an hour to read or eat a snack before requiring chores or homework, or even putting his jacket away.[39] Knowing that he has this time helps him overcome discouragement. It also gives him a predictable deadline to which he can adapt. If he has the same rest period every day, he is more likely to be ready to do small tasks afterward without complaint or hesitation. He will also have more energy and more goodwill when confronted with the next task.

Every phlegmatic child should learn to work faster and have shorter transitions as he gets older. You might have to say, "I know you like to take your time, but we need to leave in ten minutes." This acknowledges his temperament, but reminds him of the need to overcome his weaknesses. When he responds by moving faster, praise him.

Some authors say that the phlegmatic "works well under pressure."[40] This shouldn't be taken to mean that pressuring a phlegmatic will make him move. The opposite is the case. Instead, this means

---

[39] Littauer, *Parents,* 158.
[40] Tim LaHaye, *Spirit-Controlled Temperament* (La Mesa, CA: Post, 1992), 61.

that he stays calm in stressful situations and finds deadlines helpful. Deadlines enable him to set priorities and pace himself. Even in a tough work environment he'd rather stick to his work than sit and complain or speculate about the future.

Since he tends to become engrossed in his activities, set a timer to remind him to take a break.[41] Some phlegmatics may even neglect stopping to use the bathroom—with embarrassing results.

The phlegmatic dislikes taking charge of cleaning up others' messes.[42] He needs someone to stand behind him and support his decisions. Firm rules help him feel secure. If he babysits siblings, he expects you to punish those who have disobeyed him. If he disagrees with another child, he appreciates your supporting his viewpoint. He does not really want to be in authority over others or be the leader of a group project. But he does dream of doing things his way.

Passive-Aggressive Behavior

Each temperament has a different way of trying to control others. Yes, even the mild-mannered, easy-going phlegmatic desires control. He does not want to control others as the choleric does, but he insists on being free to do what is important to him. He goes with the flow, but not always in someone else's river. He has his own route to sail.

When he is assigned a task he does not like, he may use procrastination as a protest tactic.[43] If you try to push him to change, he digs in his heels. The more you nag, the more he will resist. He "quietly resent[s]" pushy people.[44] If he is phlegmatic-sanguine, the resentment may not be so quiet!

---

[41] Littauer, *Parents,* 157.
[42] Littauer, *Couples,* 206.
[43] Littauer, *Couples,* 22.
[44] Ibid., 123.

The phlegmatic runs away from conflict, but that doesn't mean he gives in. He just avoids arguing for his viewpoint. Arguing, especially when people's feelings are involved, is like a storm in his sea. He sidesteps confrontation whenever he can, and flees when he cannot prevent it. If a person with a stronger temperament forces him to act, he may withdraw emotionally. He can be the king of the cold shoulder.

The phlegmatic sometimes uses biting humor to take revenge on those he is angry with. He will act good-natured, but secretly hopes that his words sting. He may also talk about others behind their backs, while "making nice" to their faces.

Help your phlegmatic child feel safe enough to say what he really thinks and feels without criticism. Special outings alone with either parent are perfect for this. Learn to listen to your child. He may not always want to talk at the same time you want to listen. Be ready to lend him your shoulder when he needs to cry or hold his hand when he is scared. Never make light of his feelings or criticize him for them. He may refuse to ever share them with you again. It's important to him to feel safe to express his emotions, and he believes that others are constantly keeping him from doing so.

Other types of passive-aggressive behavior to watch out for are online rants; saying *yes* just to keep the peace but having no intention of following through; and pretending he doesn't hear you.

See chapter 7 for more on the phlegmatic's emotional life.

Finding a Focus

Florence Littauer writes, "I've learned that Phlegmatics are single-interest children, and our job is to locate that interest and help them develop it."[45] I think this is a symptom of the phlegmatic's desire to

---

[45] Littauer, *Parents*, 37.

stick to one path. His present interest may not turn out to be his lifelong interest. But while he is interested in one thing, he will not want to spend much energy or time on anything else. If he is forced to set aside a favorite activity for a long time, he may be reluctant to go back to it, just as he would be to start something completely new. For me, once I have moved on from a project, the thought of revisiting it almost makes me queasy. For example, once I have finished writing a book, I hate to even think about looking for typos or editing errors. When I see the end of a project nearing, I mentally leap ahead to the "done" phase. I adapt so well to *being* finished that I can't actually get done! This may be the way I have learned over the years to transition. Watch for symptoms of this behavior in your child.

Here is another example. Not long ago, I spent much of my free time for an entire year researching my dad's genealogy. Since I gave him the finished project for Christmas, I have barely looked at it again. I had been totally obsessed with it, but now my obsession lies elsewhere.

When you see that your phlegmatic child has an interest or a talent, encourage him in it. Buy him the art materials or books or camera he needs. Use this hobby to teach him the value of hard work. Hang his paintings or photos on the wall in a nice frame. Submit his stories to writing contests. Research what he is researching so that you can converse with him about it.

When he moves on to a new interest, don't press him to go back to his old love. The knowledge and skills he acquired will always be there when he is ready to return to them. Sometime later you will see him looking at his old photos again. Then be ready for the whole obsession to repeat itself.

I've always wondered if the phlegmatic may be more prone to addiction than some other temperaments. His addictions may be to seemingly inane things—sci-fi novels, baseball, or Saturday morning cartoons. Phlegmatic girls might love their American Girl dolls or girl detective book series and keep the same hairstyle most of their lives. Take care not to let this child get involved in anything that could prove harmful if done to excess.

Love is the Best Motivator

One of the best ways to motivate the phlegmatic is to show how much you love him. Don't concentrate on his accomplishments, which may not be as important to him as to you. Concentrate on his obedience, respect, likability, loyalty, and creativity. Tell him you believe in him.

The phlegmatic will be more eager to do as you ask him if he feels you appreciate him and his gifts. He needs lots of praise. He even likes flattery. Relationships are important to him. That's another reason I recommend working together. If you can find a chore the two of you do together regularly, this can build up his good will and help him to see that work can be pleasant, given the right set of circumstances. This is a great time to talk to him, give him a pat on the head, or a hug. Make sure you tell him how much you enjoy the time spent with him. Try to praise his work more often than you criticize it.

Since the phlegmatic feels that he is often overlooked and misunderstood, he is drawn to people who notice him and his gifts. He will be a loyal friend to the one who respects him.[46]

Pleasing other people is one way the phlegmatic shows affection for them. He wants to *choose* to do this, not be forced. Love cannot be forced and he knows this instinctively. He likes to surprise you with little accomplishments you didn't expect or secret obedience. But when you find out, he hopes you make a big deal out of it.

---

[46] Littauer, *Couples,* 206.

Art and Laraine Bennett suggest motivating your phlegmatic child towards virtuous acts with the words, "That would please Jesus very much."[47] Your child wants nothing more than to feel that the Almighty God is paying attention to him, values him, and is pleased with his actions.

A Word about Reward Systems

Some parents are reluctant to motivate their children with rewards or punishments. Every couple must decide for themselves whether this is right for their family. Here is my take on the subject.

I have found that reward systems can be very effective *when combined with other means of discipline.* Offering a reward to a child for behavior you do not model yourself will probably not bring about a lasting change. But if you are modeling virtue and self-control and discussing temperament issues on a regular basis, rewards can work well. On many temperament issues, I give my children points every time they overcome the temptation we are working on. When they reach a certain threshold, they can cash in their points for extra movies, fun days at school, or trips to the park. One year we decided that if they overcame their habit of leaving lights on, we would reward them with take-out. Every day when no lights were left on, they earned $.25 toward their favorite Chinese dinner. To this day, four years later, they have maintained the habit of turning lights off.

This demonstrates the power of rewards. While your child is working toward a reward, he is forming new habits. The good behavior gradually becomes more natural to him. The challenge is to wean him from the reward at the right time, so that he keeps practicing the new behavior without it.

---

[47] Bennetts, 137.

Ultimately, there is nothing wrong with desiring to benefit from good behavior. God desires that for us too. He rewards our obedience with an eternity in heaven (although we don't truly earn it). As we mature spiritually, we should begin acting out of pure love, but this takes years of spiritual growth, even for adults. If you let your child know that you do many difficult things without noticeable reward, this can plant a seed for the future. But don't lecture him about it, and don't expect him to be mature beyond his years.

CHAPTER 7

Adapting and Expressing Himself

The phlegmatic child's inertia makes it difficult for him to adapt to change. He needs time to arouse the self-motivation to adjust to new ideas and directions. When presented with a new direction, he will often resist at first. He might argue, protest, or complain at home, although in public his protests will likely be silent or passive-aggressive. At other times he refuses to act. Stopping him in the middle of a planned activity causes a similar reaction. However, if you give him enough time to adjust to the new idea, he will usually come around. In fact, the new path will become his new normal. He will end by fighting for it as strongly as he once resisted it. It will become another course he is reluctant to leave behind.

The phlegmatic needs to reflect before making decisions. Unforeseen changes throw off his equilibrium. He adapts to major reverses if given time and freedom. You cannot force him to change. Try to do so, and he may act out in other ways. His anger bursts forth when others trample on his opinion or personal freedom. Forcing tells him that he is viewed as a slave, a robot, or property, rather than a human being with dignity. He feels taken advantage of.

Recently in trying to help my son Carlo find well-written books at his reading level, I offered him Beverly Cleary's *Henry Huggins.* Too young to remember when we read Cleary's other books aloud, he glanced at the cover and proclaimed it "lame." I tried, seemingly in vain, to persuade him. We always let our kids read in bed for a while after family prayers. That night Carlo refused to tell me what he was reading. He tried to hide his book from me. Grabbing the book, I was surprised to discover he had read half a chapter of *Henry Huggins.* He even enjoyed it! Over the next few nights I heard him laughing at Henry's exploits. Then each week at the library he checked out another of Cleary's books. When it was his turn to check out a family movie, he chose Beezus and Ramona, based on the most famous series by Cleary. Given time, he had adjusted to the idea of reading *Henry Huggins* and will now be a lifetime fan.

Tendency to Go with the Flow

The phlegmatic is often described as easy-going. He accepts trivial inconveniences and has no patience with "picky" people. While other kids protest or complain about dinner options, he eats almost anything and praises the cook. Show your appreciation by letting him avoid the few foods he really hates. He lets others choose the night's entertainment, the game to play with friends or siblings, dinner discussion topics, or vacation spots. He is equally content whatever the choice. He adjusts easily to things about which he has no previous opinion, as long as they allow him to complete his plans.

Many relationship books warn against letting others make all the decisions. Authors see this as a sign of detachment from relationships. But the phlegmatic is truly neutral about most of these little things. Hamburgers or hot dogs, what's the difference? As long as he doesn't have to cook or clean or give up something he wanted to do, he's happy to go along with others. It's not abdicating responsibility. *He really does not care.*

This tendency to go with the flow becomes problematic when the culture flows against God. The phlegmatic desires to do what is right, but he dislikes making a fuss about it. If he can do good quietly, without interference, he'll be happy. He shrinks from arguing face to face for his beliefs. He fears offending or hurting others.

Public speaking gives him a chance to voice his opinion without confrontation. A shy phlegmatic may be surprisingly good behind a podium. Debate, however, is probably not where he will shine. Art and Laraine Bennett tell a hilarious story about their phlegmatic son's debate experience in *The Temperament God Gave You.*[48] He "argued" by agreeing with his opponent's stance, but taking it a step further.

The Emotional Life of Phlegmatics

The phlegmatic expresses himself when he feels comfortable and trusting.[49] He needs to be built way up before being criticized. Criticisms wound him more than any of the other temperaments.[50] He tries to be nice and accommodating and sees this as his strength. He takes criticism of his work personally.

Many authors describe the phlegmatic as a worrier. But he does not stress out in the same way as a melancholic. Problems at school, for example, will not keep him up at night. I prefer to think of him as tending towards nervousness or fear. He is often timid. He fears major personal problems, making major changes, and having to take charge of others' messes.[51] He also fears conflict, having to speak up

---

[48] Bennetts, 40-41.
[49] Ibid., 23.
[50] Ibid., 71-72.
[51] Littauer, *Couples,* 206.

in a crowd, expressing his feelings in front of unsympathetic people, being misunderstood and ignored, and anything else that rocks the boat. He might get a stomach ache at the thought of having to confront someone he disagrees with. The thought of other possible setbacks, however, he will set aside, dealing with difficulties only when he can't avoid them. He lives in the present much more than the melancholic does, hoping things will work out if he just waits long enough.

He needs peace, relaxation, attention, praise, greater self-worth, and loving motivation.[52]

The phlegmatic sees all sides of an issue. He is thus a powerful peacemaker. He objectively responds to crises without giving way to emotion. His level head is valued in tense situations. He helps opponents begin to see things from the other person's perspective.

But these qualities can also be weaknesses. Sometimes he struggles to decide which side is the right one or who has been treated unjustly. Seeing the good or the truth in both viewpoints, he finds it difficult to act. He loathes hurting anyone's feelings. He resists denying anyone to his face, even when he knows what he should do. Sometimes he bows to peer pressure, not because bad behavior attracts him, but in order to keep the peace.[53]

Since the phlegmatic does not express strong opinions, and is quiet and unemotional, he gets lost in the crowd. He is the child you inadvertently leave behind and don't even notice is missing. You may forget to include him in your plans and family discussions. Since he rarely causes trouble, you may ignore him while you focus on "more difficult" (that is, louder and more opinionated) children. The phlegmatic spends much of his life feeling unappreciated and misun-

---

[52] Ibid.
[53] Bennetts, 41.

derstood. He does not know how much people value his calm, sweet temper.

Watch for indirect ways your phlegmatic expresses himself. He may feel uncomfortable saying he loves you. Instead, he will hand-make a birthday card, use his allowance to take the family out to dinner, or even do an extra chore without being asked. This is the positive flip-side of his passive aggressiveness. He may never memorize historical dates, but know all his loved-one's birthdays.

Affection is not the only feeling he expresses indirectly. When he shares his knowledge with you, he does not do so out of pride. Sharing what he loves is the way he shares *himself.* If he enjoys a movie, he wants to watch it again with those he cares about. If he enjoys a book, he hopes his friends read it too. If he learns amazing facts in science, he tells everyone he knows. If he is working on a project, he talks about it every time he opens his mouth. He wants you to show interest, to encourage his pursuits. Doing so shows you care about *him,* even if his subject bores you.

Accept your child's feelings and opinions. Express your feelings in an appropriate way and encourage him to do the same. Never criticize him for being sad, angry, or disappointed. Instead, suggest ways he can respond to and overcome these emotions.

The phlegmatic excels at deciphering others' emotional cues, but equally excels at hiding his own feelings. More accurately, he holds his feelings so deeply within his heart, he is ignorant of them himself. They rarely reach the surface of his expressions. Emotions disturb his peace, so he tries to get along without them.

Help a young phlegmatic child draw pictures of people expressing different emotions. Then ask him how he shows the same emotions. Let him draw himself looking happy, sad, et cetera. Then when something good happens, you can ask, "Are you happy? I can't tell, because I don't see your happy face." *Don't* say, "Smile." He does not want to be told how to act, but he does want you to understand him. If he answers by saying, "Yes, I'm happy, but I don't want to smile," don't insist.

Help an older child understand his emotions by discussing those of characters in books and movies. Ask how he would feel in a similar situation. Encourage him to keep a journal in which to pour out his feelings so that he learns to know himself. This expression of emotion on paper can help him manage sadness and anger with major events in his life.

Rules and Standards

The phlegmatic wants peace, almost at any cost. This makes him favor the status quo. He wants to know and follow the rules of a game, the parameters of a project, and the standards of those in authority. When there is a standard outside himself, he readily embraces it. It gives him an anchor, so that he is not swayed to give one person an unfair advantage. Rules back him up. He can point to a rule as the reason for his decision and not feel uncomfortable about opposing another person. He is not then the bad guy. He is just the rule keeper. Rules keep him from being overrun by stronger temperaments.

He fears making exceptions to rules. Making exceptions is like opening Pandora's Box. Once he has made one, he no longer has a strict rule to fall back on and can be persuaded to make a second, eventually leading to the rules being a facade.

However, even knowing that making exceptions can cause him future problems, he sometimes allows others to bend the rules, especially if it makes his own present more peaceful. He may give in to the demands of a choleric, because he finds them too hard to resist. He may bend the rules to make a hurting person feel better, or just to put off the conflict until another day. This is a potential weakness for the phlegmatic in a leadership position. He might be especially likely to bend the rules if he has created them himself.

It is easier for him to adhere to the standards set by others, especially when he is not in charge of implementing them. His love for rules helps him to accept Church doctrine and faithfully follow authority. He rarely questions those in charge, whether teachers, parents, or employers.

Without standards he feels lost. He drifts. He doesn't know how he should act. Whom should he obey? How can he know what is best? Since he can see both sides of most questions, he has a hard time working out the details without a guide. This can paralyze him when he needs to move.

His comfort with rules explains why some people mistakenly call the phlegmatic organized. He likes to have a routine to follow when others are in charge. He knows what to expect and is not bombarded with surprises. He will follow it to the letter. However, when he is in charge, he might decide his usual routine takes too much energy and drop some items. Or his focus might change, shaking things up. When the catalyst for change comes from within him, it does not disturb him. It has often been slowly building in his psyche without his notice. But even though he can make elaborate standards for himself, once his enthusiasm wears off, he may stop following them. Any organizing that costs too much effort won't last.

At home and in school, the phlegmatic finds comfort in a predictable schedule. When giving him school assignments or chores, be specific. Make sure he understands what you expect. He can be very literal in his interpretation of your commands. If you skip a step, he won't implement it. When you give him directions to find a new destination, don't assume anything. Be completely accurate and thorough, or he is likely to get lost. He is not intuitive about such things. Likewise, if you give a phlegmatic daughter a new recipe to cook, read it through first to make sure it does not make assumptions. What you consider obvious may never enter her head. She is focused on following the written word. She considers additions to it a rejection of its authority. In all these cases, take care not to nag, pressure, or overwhelm your child.

Friendships

The phlegmatic gets along with everyone. He is not judgmental, argumentative, or cliquish. He tends to have friends in every group in school. Everyone likes him. He is a breath of fresh air for those who are tired of pride or pettiness. Yet he is rarely popular as we think of the word, simply because others forget him when he is not around. He longs for close relationships, but finds that he is often just one of many in the outer periphery of those he admires.

When two friends have opposite expectations or invite him to two events on the same day, he avoids saying *no* to either one. Then he finds himself in trouble with one or both. He lends a seemingly sympathetic ear to opposite arguments and may not even know whose side he is on, if any.

Friends can help the phlegmatic find new interests. Unmotivated on his own, he may join the speech club or go out for track because his best friend is involved.[54] His friend's involvement can help him persevere when he finds he is in over his head.

He rarely runs with the wrong crowd, because he does not like breaking rules or being disruptive.[55] But he can be afraid to say *no* when his friend invites him to a party where there will be drinking,

---

[54] Bennetts, 134.
[55] Ibid.

for example. He finds it hard to walk away from someone telling bad jokes, to stand up to bullies, or to speak up for the truth.

His tendency towards hero worship makes him vulnerable to unscrupulous people who have a surface charm. He can fall prey to cults or even child abusers. More commonly he will befriend people he does not really like because he sees that they are lonely or rejected. He may come to resent the fact that though he would like to be part of the "in" crowd, he cannot do so without hurting some of the outcasts. So he stays on the outskirts himself.

CHAPTER 8

From Servant to Servant Leader

In *A Spiritual Growth Plan for Your Choleric Child* I wrote about teaching my oldest son to become a servant leader. The phlegmatic child does not need to be taught to be a servant—if by *servant* we mean someone who wants to help the hurting. However, he needs to be taught how to lead. Without your encouragement, direction, and support, he may not reach his potential as a leader.

This potential is often overlooked by others. One vocation where many phlegmatic men do well is in the priesthood. Phlegmatics also succeed as teachers, counselors, spiritual directors, or police officers.

While acknowledging this, we should recognize that the phlegmatic will not lead in the same way as the choleric. Each temperament has its own leadership style. He is a good authority one on one with other adults or over a group of children. In these situations, his authority is rarely questioned by someone on his own level. He is less apt to second-guess himself or become involved in conflict.

As a priest, for example, he has an education in theology and philosophy that others rarely match. Besides that, he has the grace of the Sacrament of Holy Orders. He alone in the parish can consecrate the Eucharist and give absolution. Only he and any deacon can preach homilies. If he has a spiritual vision for his parish, he can excel in leading people closer to Christ, while letting lay people handle many of the administrative duties he is not as good at.

The phlegmatic loves to lead by modeling. To teach others to be patient, he shows them the way and hopes they follow his example. In this way, a holy phlegmatic can change the world. Many saints who were doorkeepers for their religious communities were phlegmatics. Unsuited for menial or intellectual work, they became symbols of the order to the outside world. Time and again, the sick, the troubled, and the hurting gathered around these lowly souls, finding healing, counseling, and the touch of God. Among the doorkeeper saints are St. Faustina Kowalska, St. Andre of Montreal, and St. Alfonso Rodriguez. Venerable Solanus Casey also led others to Christ as a doorkeeper.

Teaching the Phlegmatic to Lead

Good leaders are organized, know how to make decisions, recognize and make use of the gifts of those under them, and persevere in the midst of setbacks. They make their goals and expectations clear. They learn from their mistakes, rather than being paralyzed by them. Some of these characteristics come naturally to the phlegmatic. Others challenge him.

The phlegmatic excels at understanding others. He is keyed in to gestures and facial expressions that may contradict another's words. He rarely makes enemies. Thus, another characteristic way for him to lead is by bringing out the best in others. His gentle way of pointing out others' mistakes is nonthreatening. He makes peace between rivals. He teaches people with opposite perspectives how to listen to each other. He makes a mob into a team, or even a family.

But in order to do this, he must first gain others' respect. Willingness to work hard, to stand up for himself and others, and to speak his mind are essential. We will discuss some of these things more fully in chapter 9 on the spiritual works of mercy.

Organizational Skills

I have read several books and articles about the temperaments that call the phlegmatic *organized*. This may be a misunderstanding of his adherence to rules. Even with a strong melancholic streak I am not the least bit organized. My motto of organization has long been: a place for everything and nothing in its place. Although I enjoy putting things in order (if I have no more pressing matter to attend to), I do not enjoy keeping them that way. It is much faster to place a paper in a pile on my desk than to find the right file for it. Perhaps this misunderstanding also comes from the phlegmatic's command of the project he is focused on. He masters it so thoroughly, others assume he is very organized in his approach. Instead, he has learned to overcome the handicaps of his disorganization.

Some basic organizational skills are important for the phlegmatic to be able to excel, however. Here are some simple guidelines that can help you teach your child organization:

- Remember that he gets overwhelmed easily.
- Implement one step at a time.
- Look at the big picture, rather than insisting on many details.
- Let him use the system that works best for him.

If you want your child to keep his room neat, for example, keep your expectations low. Work on having him put his clothes away immediately. While he is making this a habit, don't nag him about books or toys on the floor. Don't expect him to keep his shelves or dresser neat. If you can get him to keep his clothes in order, you have won a great battle. Celebrate with him. Praise him for his progress. Yes, it is a very little thing, but life is made up of little things. Better a little success than a big failure.

Another small step could be smoothing out his bedspread without worrying about minor lumps in the layers under it. Large tubs in the closet can be toy dumpsters to facilitate clean up, but don't let them become catch-alls for papers and library books. Likewise, if he is in charge of doing the dishes, let him keep the clean dishes in the dishwasher until he needs them to set the table, for example. Aim for keeping the counters and sink relatively clear, rather than having everything neatly stacked behind cupboard doors.

In all this, you are requiring progress (which all of us need to continually work on), but not expecting perfection (which the phlegmatic may never attain).

The most important aspect of being organized is not having the perfect system, but following through. Try having him check off chores on a chart or assignments in a notebook. Allow him to do the minimum necessary to keep track of his activities. Let him mold the system to his personality. Expect to remind him often at the beginning.

Hang a classroom or family calendar where he will see it often. Encourage him to write down his own dentist appointments, sporting events, and play dates, working with him until he is old enough to do this by himself without errors. Knowing what is approaching helps him adapt and feel less overwhelmed.

If you homeschool, try giving each child a three-ring binder to keep his papers in. We also each have an expensive portfolio of our best art projects. As your child reaches the teen years, teach him to create digital folders to keep track of his assignments. Of course, you will have to monitor this, so you don't end up in trouble with your state for not keeping all the mandated records!

Following a similar routine daily and weekly not only helps your child do the right task at the right time without forgetting or hesitating. It also makes him feel more comfortable, because you are drawing the boundary lines he desires.

Telling the Truth

Sweet as the phlegmatic can be, he also falls prey to the temptation to lie and even to cheat. His lies do not stem so much from pride as they do from a desire for peace. He does not like to be put on the spot. He loathes conflict. If smoothing over the truth or putting off a difficult confrontation can make the present more peaceful, he is liable to choose the easy way.

Teach him that conflict has a purpose. Although it brings temporary discomfort, long term it can be for his good. If you make it easy for him to express his feelings, protect him from the anger of choleric siblings, and teach him how to stand up for himself, much of the lying will disappear.

Model truthfulness.

The phlegmatic knows his weaknesses. Teaching him to say *I'm sorry* makes him more likely to express uncomfortable feelings. Inculcate this habit early. Be understanding when he sins or errs. Otherwise he may be ashamed of falling short, which could lead to dishonesty. Let him know that you love him no matter what. Show him you value him as a person and that honesty is more important than instant perfection.

Understanding that a temptation to fudge the truth is part of his temperament does not mean you can excuse it. Lying and cheating are not acceptable. Satan is the father of lies.[56] God is truth. To become the holy person God designed him to be, your child must be able to speak truthfully.

Experts suggest that you avoid asking questions to which your child will be tempted to lie. They call this a *set-up question*. For example, if you find a broken dish in the kitchen and suspect your phlegmatic child, don't ask all the kids, "Who broke this?" He will be tempted to remain silent or to chime in *Not me* with everyone else. By answering this way, he is practicing lying. He is forming a bad habit. You want to form the habit of speaking the truth instead.

So how can you handle such a situation? Think about what the child did wrong and what he should have done instead. Then address the behavior, rather than focusing on the fact that he did not tell you about it. You could ask, "What do you think you should do when you break a dish?" Show him how to take care of the problem. He might still play dumb, but at least you have not set him up for an outright lie. If he answers with a shrug, say, "Come with me and I'll show you." Then lead him to the kitchen and guide him through the process of cleaning up the mess or do it yourself as his age requires.

If you suspect he is lying about something, tell him, "That doesn't sound like the truth to me." Explain that many people are tempted to lie when they are afraid, but that in your family no one has to fear the consequences of honesty.[57] If he lies to cover up for mistakes or bad behavior, remind him that you are imperfect too and that you will always love him, no matter what he does. Tell him you can be a better help and support to him if you know what he is struggling with. You want to help him grow closer to God.

---

[56] John 8:44.
[57] See Jane Nelsen, Lynn Lott & H. Stephen Glenn, "Lying," *Positive Discipline,* http://www.positivediscipline.com/articles/lying.html (accessed November 14, 2015).

Of course, lies must still be punished so that they don't happen again. But use positive rather than negative reinforcement as your main weapon for this child.

Being Assertive

When a phlegmatic hears the word *assertive,* he imagines a bossy, opinionated person that won't let him be himself. But what does the word really mean? *Psychology Today* says:

> Demonstrating assertiveness means there's no question where you stand, no matter the topic. Cognitively, to be assertive implies a lack of anxious thoughts in light of stress. Behaviorally, assertiveness is all about asking for what you want in a manner that respects others. Assertive people don't shy away from defending their points of view or goals, or from trying to influence others. In terms of affect, assertiveness means reacting to positive and negative emotions without aggression or resorting to passivity.[58]

Let's break that down into two parts, the cognitive and the behavioral. The peaceful phlegmatic loves living stress-free. Assertiveness training helps him achieve this. Learning to attack his problems head-on helps him move on from the stress they cause. Instead of dreading speaking up, he can simply act. Then he has nothing more to dread.

But how can you help him take that first step in the face of his fear?

As always, modeling is imperative. Show your child how to speak up for himself and his beliefs by practicing it yourself. When you receive setbacks at work, have disagreements with your family, or experience bad customer service, act assertively. Tell your child

---

[58] "All About Assertiveness," *Psychology Today,* https://www.psychologytoday.com/basics/assertiveness (accessed November 14, 2015).

the steps you take. Explain how you acted respectfully, but firmly. Tell him how you persisted in the face of opposition. Especially share the positive results of your assertiveness.

If he feels free to express his emotions without criticism (see chapter 7), he will not be so anxious about speaking out.

Teach him phrases he can use to begin speaking about his differences with others. For example:

- The way I see it...
- My experience is...
- I have always thought (or felt)...
- In our family, we...

These phrases soften "the blow" of a dissenting opinion. They allow him to assert himself without sounding arrogant or close-minded.

If his opponent rejects what he has to say, teach him to clarify his viewpoint and ask the other person for clarification, rather than insisting he won't budge.[59] The phlegmatic tends to be all or nothing in discussions. He either gives in completely to the other person, or he rejects everything his opponent says, often silently. He thinks that speaking up will lead to arguing, yelling, or having his feelings invalidated. Although he will always feel some discomfort when he is not in full agreement with another person, help him use his good listening skills to come to an understanding. Help him look for a way both parties' desires can be satisfied.

Form these habits by practicing as a family. Practice asking questions such as:

- Why do you feel that way?

---

[59] See Leon F. Seltzer, PhD, "How—and How Not—to Stand Up for Yourself," *Psychology Today*, https://www.psychologytoday.com/blog/evolution-the-self/201209/how-and-how-not-stand-yourself (accessed November 14, 2015)

- I hear you saying... Is that correct?
- Why is this important to you?
- What's your key need in this situation?

Regarding the last question, help your child identify his key needs first, so he can better understand others. Temperament studies can help. Other phlegmatics primarily desire peace. Melancholics desire perfection. Cholerics desire control. Sanguines desire fun and affection. So, is your child putting off making a decision in exchange for temporary peace? Is his opponent doing something similar? How can they achieve peace while still moving forward? Can he agree with the melancholic to focus on making one small issue better, aiming towards perfection on it while setting other aspects of the problem aside for later? If the phlegmatic has only one thing to work on, he won't feel overburdened and his hyper-focus can help him achieve what the melancholic is asking for. For conflicts with the choleric, have him find out what his opponent's over-all goal is, then agree to help him towards it in a way that suits his own temperament. Here is a fictional exchange to illustrate.

Choleric: Get your mess out of my room.

Phlegmatic: You mean my stuffed animals?

Choleric: Yes, you've made a huge mess in my room.

Phlegmatic: I'll take care of them after I finish this art project.

Choleric: I want them out of here now.

Phlegmatic: But I'm in the middle of this. Is there a reason you can't wait ten minutes? Do you really need me to hurry?

Choleric: I know that if you don't do it now, you'll forget and it will never get done.

Phlegmatic: Let me see... I have an idea. Why don't you set the timer on the stove for ten minutes? I'll work on my project until the timer rings. Then I'll clean up my animals.

Choleric: Fine.

Problem solved! Both parties got what they wanted. Of course, the phlegmatic's drawback is that he is slow to come up with solutions. Often he'll think of the perfect answer ten minutes after he has left the conversation. But with practice he can learn what works and use the same suggestions repeatedly.

Here's a second exchange, this time with a melancholic.

Melancholic: Look at the lumps in your bed! Can't you make it smoother?

Phlegmatic: Why? I'm just going to mess it up again when I go to sleep.

Melancholic: But in the meantime it looks awful.

Phlegmatic: Why do you care that it looks awful? It's my bed. If I don't care, why should you?

Melancholic: Because we share a room. My friends are coming over, and I'm embarrassed to have it look so bad.

Phlegmatic: Oh, okay. I'll take care of it in a minute. (When the melancholic sibling isn't looking, he smooths the major lumps in his bed without lifting the comforter.)

Again, problem solved. Minimal work for the phlegmatic and a melancholic sibling saved from embarrassment.

If the whole family, including the parents, work on better conflict resolution skills together, the atmosphere for asserting oneself will be less threatening. You can all practice without others thinking you are weird for asking questions, or refusing to listen to your suggestions. The more often the phlegmatic resolves a problem in an amicable manner, the more confidence he will have in his assertiveness skills. He will become less timid about speaking up outside the family.

A (somewhat) organized phlegmatic who is not afraid to be honest or assertive can make a great servant leader. In the next chapter, we'll see how he can practice servant leadership with the spiritual works of mercy.

CHAPTER 9

The Spiritual Works of Mercy

Y our phlegmatic child sympathizes with the poor and the hurting. He dreams of feeding the hungry or tending the sick. Find opportunities for him to live this dream while young and enthusiastic. If he puts it off, he may later be reluctant to make the effort it costs. Practicing the works of mercy helps him work on his leadership skills while serving the Lord.

The corporal works of mercy are

- feeding the hungry
- giving drink to the thirsty
- clothing the naked
- sheltering the homeless
- visiting the sick
- visiting the imprisoned (formerly "ransoming the captive")
- burying the dead

These are taken from a passage in the Gospels concerning the Last Judgment:

> When the Son of man comes in his glory, and all the angels with him, then he will sit on his glorious throne. Before him will be gathered all the nations, and he will separate them one from another as a shepherd separates the sheep from the goats, and he will place the sheep at his right hand, but the goats at the left. Then

the King will say to those at his right hand, "Come, O blessed of my Father, inherit the kingdom prepared for you from the foundation of the world; for I was hungry and you gave me food, I was thirsty and you gave me drink, I was a stranger and you welcomed me, I was naked and you clothed me, I was sick and you visited me, I was in prison and you came to me."

Then the righteous will answer him, "Lord, when did we see thee hungry and feed thee, or thirsty and give thee drink? And when did we see thee a stranger and welcome thee, or naked and clothe thee? And when did we see thee sick or in prison and visit thee?"

And the King will answer them, "Truly, I say to you, as you did it to one of the least of these my brethren, you did it to me."

Then he will say to those at his left hand, "Depart from me, you cursed, into the eternal fire prepared for the devil and his angels; for I was hungry and you gave me no food, I was thirsty and you gave me no drink, I was a stranger and you did not welcome me, naked and you did not clothe me, sick and in prison and you did not visit me."

Then they also will answer, "Lord, when did we see thee hungry or thirsty or a stranger or naked or sick or in prison, and did not minister to thee?"

Then he will answer them, "Truly, I say to you, as you did it not to one of the least of these, you did it not to me." And they will go away into eternal punishment, but the righteous into eternal life.[60]

For the phlegmatic who is less energetic or has fewer opportunities to exercise the corporal works of mercy, the spiritual works of mercy are a perfect way for him to spread the Gospel.

They are

- instructing the ignorant

---

[60] Mt 25:31-46.

- counseling the doubtful
- admonishing sinners
- bearing wrongs patiently
- forgiving offenses willingly
- comforting the afflicted
- praying for the living and the dead

These works of mercy are available to everyone, physically weak as well as strong, those living in the country, as well as in the city or town. In the following pages we will break down each of these as ways to help the phlegmatic grow as a person and a Christian. With each section, I also suggest a male and a female saint to study who exemplified the work of mercy.

Instructing the Ignorant

Instructing the ignorant means teaching others, especially about the faith. The phlegmatic is naturally compassionate. He wants to help people. Many school teachers are phlegmatics. Many public speakers are phlegmatic-melancholics. Teachers have a heart for people. How can you help your phlegmatic explore this work of mercy?

In order to teach, your child must first learn. This can actually motivate him in school. He can't pass on to others what he doesn't know himself. One potential problem is that the phlegmatic tends to put off things that are difficult. He might think that he can start working hard on academics in high school, or next year, or next month. So, can you use this to motivate him right now?

If you homeschool, encourage him to teach younger siblings. Girls are especially good at this. You can start by having the phlegmatic read books aloud to a toddler, then later write letters for the younger child to copy. He can teach his sibling the names of colors, how to use a scissors and glue, and later practice with phonics and math flashcards.

Assign him oral reports. Teach him to be a good public speaker, to be confident, to have good posture, to look at his audience, to be coherent and entertaining. Start with informative speeches. As he gets older, he can learn to give persuasive speeches and personal experience talks as well.

School plays and choir are also ways he can build confidence in front of a crowd.

Good writing skills help him teach the ignorant. Many of the bloggers I know are phlegmatics like myself. They can teach others the faith while sitting in the comfort of their home office. Not having to face readers, a phlegmatic is bolder online than in person. He can take the time to answer comments charitably as well as thoroughly.

Many fine columnists or book authors are phlegmatics. If the phlegmatic loves a writing project, he will eagerly see it through. Encourage your child to express himself through creative writing, journaling, and written reports. Teach him good grammar.

Above all, immerse him in the Bible, church history, and the writings of the saints. The more he loves the faith, the more eager he will be to share it with others.

Saints to study: St. Justin Martyr or St. Elizabeth Ann Seaton.

Counseling the Doubtful

Counseling the doubtful means helping those who are not sure how they should act to make the right decision—especially deciding what God wants them to do at any given time. The phlegmatic excels at giving counsel to others. He advises those who ask to follow the

Church and the moral law. He listens to their concerns. He encourages and supports them in doing the right thing.

However, when a person must choose between two things that can both be good or right, the phlegmatic hesitates to counsel one or the other. If no rule is being broken, no one obviously being hurt, he sees the good in both sides. By developing decision-making skills and showing others how to use them, he can help them discern what God desires them to do, without presuming himself to know God's will on prudential matters.

Here are some steps you can help him practice as he moves into the teen years. This eight-step process should be accompanied by prayer. At each step, the phlegmatic should ask the Holy Spirit to lead him to the best decision. He should record the results of each step.

1. Why must you make a decision?

Be clear about what you hope to accomplish. How long do you have to decide? What are the consequences of putting off the decision?

2. Brainstorm a list of possible choices.

List as many possibilities as you can think of without being too critical. You will eliminate bad choices in the following steps.

3. What short-term difference could your decision make?

Remember that some decisions that are good in the long term can make life more difficult for a short time. How much short-term discomfort are you willing to endure to meet a long-term goal?

4. What long-term goals could your decision affect?

Think about how this decision will make a difference in your life six months, a year, or ten years from now. How might your decision affect the people who are most important in your life? How could your vocation, your relationship with God, your life's work, or your favorite pastimes be affected?

5. Decide which options meet your long-term goals. Eliminate the rest.

Remember, what makes you comfortable in the short term is not necessarily the best long-term choice. (This step is key for the phlegmatic, who stubbornly ignores future problems if doing so makes the present more comfortable.)

6. Order the remaining items as they meet your short-term goals.

7. Eliminate any items that are unrealistic to implement.

Is any choice too expensive, too difficult, or out of bounds for someone your age? Would you really follow through with your choice?

8. Choose the best remaining course of action.

Always have a back-up plan in case you cannot go forward with your decision, or in case it does not work out. For major decisions, you should also re-evaluate your choice periodically, to make sure it is still the right decision.

Saints to study: St. John Vianney or St. Joan of Arc.

Admonishing Sinners

To admonish sinners means to gently and lovingly point out to someone that his life is not in line with the Gospel.

Admonishing sinners may be the hardest of the spiritual works of mercy for the phlegmatic to practice. When he sees someone acting immorally, he tries to give that person the benefit of the doubt. He makes excuses for the offender, looks at things from the other's perspective, or assumes ignorance. When he is convinced that the other person has unrepentant sin on his soul, he feels compassion, knowing that this sin could keep the person from intimacy with Christ. He desires to repair the relationship with God. He wants the other person to be truly happy. However, he resists arguing. He recoils from embarrassing anyone. Nor does he want others to think he sees himself as better or holier than them. He is unlikely to be a busy-body who is overly concerned with others' sins.

How can we encourage the phlegmatic to speak up, so that he can draw others to God's love and mercy?

The Baltimore Catechism asks, "When are we bound to admonish the sinner?" The answer:

> A. We are bound to admonish the sinner when the following conditions are fulfilled:
> 1. When his fault is a mortal sin;
> 2. When we have authority or influence over him, and
> 3. When there is reason to believe that our warning will not make him worse instead of better.[61]

So, if someone commits a minor fault, we are not morally bound to point it out. That does not mean we should necessarily ignore it. It

---

[61] No. 814.

depends on our relationship with the sinner and other circumstances.

Note the third condition. If the sinner is highly unlikely to repent because of our words, we are not morally bound to speak. As my spiritual director once explained to me, the more times a sinner hears warnings, the more responsible he becomes for continuing in his sin. Thus, our words of admonishment could actually increase his responsibility and punishment. If someone is living a public life of sin and has been warned before, unless we are very close to him, in authority over him, or feel a special inspiration from God to speak, we do best to remain silent. On the other hand, we can only predict what someone's reaction to our words will be, not know it with certainty. We may be the first person bold enough to confront a sinner, or have just the right words to say. We are not bound, however, to speak up concerning every mortal sin that we hear about, or we might have no time for anything else.

Every admonition of the sinner requires prayer and reflection.

As a child in your household, the phlegmatic may never have an occasion in which he is bound to admonish a sinner. But he is likely to have many as an adult. Parents, religious superiors, counselors, confessors, and even close friends can be called upon to caution others against sin.

Jesus instructed his disciples:

> If your brother sins against you, go and tell him his fault, between you and him alone. If he listens to you, you have gained your brother. But if he does not listen, take one or two others along with you, that every word may be confirmed by the evidence of two or three witnesses. If he refuses to listen to them, tell it to the church; and if he refuses to listen even to the church, let him be to you as a Gentile and a tax collector. Truly, I say to you, whatever you bind on earth shall be bound in heaven, and whatever you loose on earth shall be loosed in heaven. Again I say to you, if two of you agree on earth about anything they ask, it will be done for

them by my Father in heaven. For where two or three are gathered in my name, there am I in the midst of them. (Mt 18:15-20)

This saying of Jesus concerns someone who sins against you. Sometimes it is necessary to heal a relationship that has been damaged by sin, even if the sin was not mortal. Tension exists between this work of mercy and bearing wrongs patiently. Teach your phlegmatic child that bearing wrongs and forgiving offenses do not preclude admonishing the sinner.

If he speaks up once, he has usually done all God requires. For serious matters that are affecting more than just himself, he should recruit others and ultimately the Church to back him up. He is not responsible for the results. In many cases, his admonition will fall on deaf ears. Then all he can do is continue to pray for the sinner's conversion.

In order to effectively admonish the sinner, we must recognize our own weaknesses. The phlegmatic is well aware of his shortcomings. He does not push himself forward or seek to dominate others. He seldom shrinks from going to confession, even face to face. Like Jesus himself, he sympathizes with the weak, because he has experienced weakness.[62]

Another aid to admonishing the sinner may be more problematic: practicing what he preaches. The phlegmatic often fails to follow through on what he intends to do. He might have insight into the best way to act, but find himself too weak. He counsels or admonishes others, and needs them to reciprocate.

The phlegmatic finds strength and motivation in words such as these:

My brethren, if any one among you wanders from the truth and someone brings him back, let him know that whoever brings back

---

[62] See Heb 2:18.

> a sinner from the error of his way will save his soul from death
> and will cover a multitude of sins. (Jas 5:19-20)

His act of admonishing the sinner might have eternal consequences. Encourage him to think about seeing in heaven those whom he has helped turn back to God. How he will rejoice with them! A contemporary Christian song from the 1980s expresses this beautifully and I encourage you to share it with your phlegmatic child. It's called Thank You for Giving to the Lord, by Ray Boltz. You can listen to it here: http://www.youtube.com/watch?v=d-3BJrG79IA

You can also read and discuss these Scripture passages with your child:

- Jonah (especially the portion about Ninevah's repentance)
- Acts 2:14-41
- 2 Samuel 12:1-15 (for teens and older)

Saints to study: St. James the Just or St. Catherine of Siena.

Bearing Wrongs Patiently

Unlike admonishing the sinner, this work of mercy always regards an offense against oneself or someone dear to you. Jesus instructs in the Sermon on the Mount:

> But I say to you, Do not resist one who is evil. But if any one
> strikes you on the right cheek, turn to him the other also; and if
> any one would sue you and take your coat, let him have your
> cloak as well; and if any one forces you to go one mile, go with
> him two miles. (Mt 5:39)

This is one of the "hard" sayings of Jesus. What did he mean?

The phlegmatic risks thinking he is performing this work of mercy when he is really just avoiding conflict. He might allow others to use and abuse him, rather than standing up for himself. How can he tell he is performing a virtuous act rather than just running away from something he doesn't want to face?

One way to discern is to ask himself how comfortable the act makes him. If it just comes automatically, he is likely behaving according to his temperament. If it requires sacrifice, prayer, and repeated acts of the will, it's more likely a true work of mercy. A second measure looks at the phlegmatic's private behavior. Is he grumbling to you, his siblings, or his best friend? Then he's not being patient, even if he puts up a good public show of it.

St. Thomas Aquinas interprets Jesus' words this way:

> Holy Scripture must be understood in the light of what Christ and the saints have actually practiced. Christ did not offer His other cheek, nor Paul either. Thus to interpret the injunction of the Sermon on the Mount *literally* is to misunderstand it. This injunction signifies rather the readiness of the soul to bear, if it be *necessary*, such things and worse, without bitterness against the attacker. This readiness our Lord showed, when He gave up His body to be crucified. That response of the Lord was useful, therefore, for our instruction.[63]

In other words, if we can resist evil, if we can protect ourselves from another person's literal or figurative blows without seeking revenge, we should. Jesus did not turn the other cheek when the high priest struck him, but admonished him for his sin, which broke the Law of Moses. Then Jesus bore scourging and being crowned with thorns patiently. He forgave those who crucified him. At each point, he had to discern what action would further the Father's purpose.

As I said earlier, bearing wrongs patiently sometimes seems to conflict with admonishing the sinner. The phlegmatic should learn to ask, *What would benefit my opponent most? My remaining silent or my speaking up?* If someone commits a minor sin against him—one that

---

[63] *In John* 18, lect. 4, 2.

does not greatly damage their relationship—bearing it without comment is often best. Sins that fall outside the three conditions for admonishing the sinner are also often best overlooked.

Wrongs are not always sins. They can also be misunderstandings or errors of judgment. Does charity or justice demand that the phlegmatic explain or defend himself? Or will silence better accomplish God's will? These are questions you can help your phlegmatic child explore.

The phlegmatic can be an example of obedience to the command of Jesus, as long as he is truly acting out of love for God, not fear of man.

Saints to study: King David or St. Bernadette of Lourdes.

Forgiving Offenses Willingly

Forgiving offenses willingly goes one step beyond bearing wrongs patiently and covers wider ground. Often others sin against us inadvertently. They don't always give us an opportunity for turning the other cheek. But they do always give us a chance to forgive. Jesus, as well as many martyrs, forgave those who put him to death. How can the phlegmatic child begin practicing this work of mercy?

From his earliest days, teach your child to say *I'm sorry* and *I forgive you.* Practice with gestures as well as words: a hug, a kiss, a handshake. Model this work of mercy by scorning grudges against others, especially your family and relatives. Try to discipline out of love, not anger. Don't let necessary punishment appear to be revenge. Once you have meted out punishment, put the incident behind you. Don't talk about your child's mistake with others. Don't remind him of it unless necessary for his growth.

Read the Lord's Prayer with your child in the context of the Sermon on the Mount, including these verses:

> If you forgive others their transgressions, your heavenly Father will forgive you. But if you do not forgive others, neither will your Father forgive your transgressions. (Mt 6:14-15)

Another important passage to read is the parable of the unforgiving servant.[64] Discuss why the Our Father is prayed before receiving Communion at Mass.

Sometimes the phlegmatic will seem to forgive others on the surface, but he will not realize how deeply he has been hurt. Help your child see that pretending he has not been wronged is not the same thing as forgiving. In order to forgive, he must acknowledge that someone has sinned against him, yet decide to move beyond his hurt out of love for Christ. For this reason, prohibit him from saying *It's okay* when someone offends him. Sin is not okay. Intentionally hurting others is not okay. But it is forgivable.

Saints to study: St. Stephen or St. Maria Goretti.

Comforting the Afflicted

The phlegmatic shines at comforting the afflicted. His ears are opened to every sorrow. He listens, he encourages. Sometimes he even "weep[s] with those who weep."[65] He is often more hurt by the offenses committed against his loved ones than those committed against himself. He can be sadder at their loss than his own.

Help your phlegmatic child show sympathy through his expressions and gestures. A comforting arm, an encouraging smile—he often longs to show sympathy this way, but is too timid or self-conscious. Teach him to be a more active listener. Prompt him to ask questions and show sympathy with words.

---

[64] Mt 18:21-35.
[65] Rom 12:15.

He has a tendency to respond to someone's sad story with a story of his own. This is his sideways manner of showing emotion. But the hurting person can interpret this as being unsympathetic, of thinking more about himself than the one hurting. And he can easily start to focus on his own story, rather than actively engaging with the story of the other. Sitting silently and patiently listening is often the greatest comfort we can extend when someone's sorrow is fresh. It is so easy to offend instead of comfort! Friends and family will appreciate the phlegmatic's loyal, sympathetic silence.

On the other hand, the story of his afflictions can be powerful in leading other hurting people to find comfort in God, if shared gently at the right time. Usually it is best to wait until some time has passed since the hurt occurred. In the meantime, he can pray for his friend, and gently suggest praying *with* him.

Comforting the afflicted can cross over into the corporal works of mercy. A note, a card, a bouquet of flowers, a phone call let the hurting person know you are still thinking of him. Little acts of love at difficult times will be remembered forever.

Listening to your child's sorrows, even ones that may seem trivial to you, can teach him to be more sympathetic to others. Don't be callous with the things that bother him.

Saints to study: St. (Padre) Pio of Pietrelcina or St. Brigid.

Praying for the Living and the Dead

This is a wonderful work of mercy that almost anyone can do. Several years ago, we added to our nightly list of people we ask God to bless, *All the people waiting to get into heaven.* I wanted to ensure that the boys knew who we were praying for and why. Carlo was only three at the time. I didn't want him, or his older brothers, rattling off, *All the souls in Purgatory,* while having no idea what Purgatory was. So we put it in simple terms. Every child wants to go to heaven, and every child experiences waiting when he would like to have something immediately. The boys could thus sympathize with those they were praying for, even if they did not yet fully understand. Now that my youngest is a preschooler, we will probably start using the word *Purgatory* in our evening prayers soon.

We began praying for the souls in Purgatory in November, the special month of the suffering souls. By the end of the month, it had become such a habit, I decided we should continue. Once in a while I remind the boys that those souls they pray for now will in turn pray for them. It excites us all to think about our connection with those who have already died. Someday, we will see these souls in heaven and have a special relationship with them.

Praying for the dead also helps the phlegmatic to look beyond his own desires and needs and those of his loved ones. As I have mentioned before, the phlegmatic can be seen as selfish because he does not easily think about other people unless prompted. Praying for the unknown dead helps him practice charity.

Do you have a purse, drawer, or Bible full of prayer cards from funerals? Let your phlegmatic child start a collection. Encourage him to pray for at least one of them each day, in whatever way he chooses. This can be his special mission.

Praying for the living can also be a special mission. Many members of contemplative orders spend their lives praying for others. Your child doesn't have to wait until he enters the cloister to begin. Does your parish have a sister parish overseas? Does your diocese have a foreign mission? Other ideas for his prayer mission could be seminarians, children in a particular country that you learn about as a family, people with a specific disease or disability, the local homeless, or the unborn.

Saints to study: St. Vincent Ferrer or St. Monica.

CHAPTER 10

An Atmosphere for Learning

The atmosphere of your home will affect your child's spiritual life. As a phlegmatic, he needs a quiet, peaceful home to function at his best. Such a home also provides the perfect atmosphere for the prayerful life you want to foster in your child.

How can you bring Catholic culture into your home? At one time in history, the Catholic faith was the greatest power behind western culture. The world's finest artists, architects, musicians, and writers all came from a Catholic worldview. They painted cathedrals, composed Mass settings, built St. Peter's Basilica, and wrote about heaven, hell, and Purgatory. Sadly, our secularized world now produces profane works and calls them art.

Experiencing Transcendent Beauty

Beauty appeals to the imagination. It can move your child to a greater desire for and love of God. An appreciation for beauty distinguishes humans from lower animals. The beauty of a sunset does not move a dog. A line from a hymn cannot stir the heart of a rabbit.

Created "in the image of God," man also expresses the truth of his relationship with God the Creator by the beauty of his artistic works. Indeed, art is a distinctively human form of expression; beyond the search for the necessities of life which is common to all living creatures, art is a freely given superabundance of the human being's inner riches. Arising from talent given by the Creator and from man's own effort, art is a form of practical wisdom, uniting knowledge and skill, to give form to the truth of reality in a language accessible to sight or hearing. To the extent that it is inspired by truth and love of beings, art bears a certain likeness to God's activity in what he has created. Like any other human activity, art is not an absolute end in itself, but is ordered to and ennobled by the ultimate end of man. [66]

Your phlegmatic child does not just have an intellect and a will. He also has an imagination, given to him by God to be another way to lead him towards divine union. The imagination does not remain empty. It seeks material to feed upon.

The phlegmatic child hungers for beauty. True beauty brings him feelings of peace and contentment. You can help satisfy this desire by filling your home with religious objects. Try to find works by the masters or truly great contemporary artists. A Bible with beautiful, rather than cartoonish, illustrations can also fill this role. Listening to hymns, especially during the Christmas and Easter seasons, provides a holy backdrop for your daily activities. You can also celebrate your child's feast days with traditional dishes or a special dessert. Supply him with high-quality books to read, both fiction and nonfiction.

The phlegmatic often loves to draw or paint. Make sure he has time and materials to pursue this love.

---

[66] CCC, no. 2051.

Regulating Mass Media

Your phlegmatic child will easily become addicted to TV or video games. Once he starts, he will not want to stop. He can become a couch potato. Help him form the habits for a healthy adult life.

Monitor the level of immorality he views on the screen. The phlegmatic wants to be good, but he can be swayed by sins of the flesh. It is your duty to ensure he is not faced with too much information too soon.

An instruction for parents from the Diocese of La Crosse, Wisconsin, says of children who have not yet reached puberty:

> In this stage, parents are *recommended* to withhold sexually explicit information that may interrupt a child's right to innocence. Thus, you must monitor and limit the influence of mass media on your children as well as scrutinize what other external pressures may be present.[67]

Respect this time, which the Church calls *the latency period.*

The Internet, smartphones, and other electronic devices pose similar challenges. Used correctly, they can help the phlegmatic express himself freely without fear. But they can also become his primary focus in life to the point of obsession. They can become outlets for passive-aggressive behavior, and reinforce his tendencies to ignore others. Ask yourself, *Does he really need this? Or am I giving in to pressure from him or from people outside our family? Can he be trusted to finish his chores and homework with digital distractions?* Remember, he has his whole life to surf the web. He has a few short years as a child in your household. Cherish those years. Don't assume that what is good for adults is also good for children.

---

[67] *Hey Parents—Teach Them About Real Love! Parent Handbook on Human Sexuality* (2003), no. 5. Emphasis in original.

Do you know that every sensory stimulus creates a memory? In fact, therapists now use sensory stimulation to help strengthen the memories of Alzheimer's patients. Recall how a smell can transport you back to childhood, or how you can still recite car commercials you saw thirty years ago. Every memory in turn is a potential distraction from what is important in life. When people fill their minds with sights and sounds, distraction in prayer follows. Kids are particularly susceptible to this, because their memories are so vivid.

The American Academy of Pediatrics, anything but a conservative organization, says:

> Studies have shown that excessive media use can lead to attention problems, school difficulties, sleep and eating disorders, and obesity. In addition, the Internet and cell phones can provide platforms for illicit and risky behaviors.[68]

They recommend limiting children's use of all electronic media combined to two hours a day. Children under two, they say, should not be exposed to digital media or television at all.

It is much easier to limit media use from the start than to curtail overuse. And of course as your child enters his later teen years, you may decide that more media exposure is appropriate. Be very prayerful as you discern what is right for your child at various ages.

This is another area where you must lead by your example. If you are constantly texting, on the Internet, or in front of the TV, your children will likely behave the same way.

For nearly a century, great Catholic thinkers have cautioned against an overuse or abuse of mass media, including Edith Stein (St. Teresa Benedicta of the Cross), Marshall McLuhan, the Council Fathers of Vatican II, Pope St. John Paul II, Cardinal Avery Dulles, and Peter Kreeft. As a person grows in intimacy with God, one of the

---

[68] "Media and Children," www.aap.org/en-us/advocacy-and-policy/aap-health-initiatives/Pages/Media-and-Children.aspx.

purifications he must submit to is purification of the memory. All images that don't lead him closer to Christ will have to go. This can be a long and painful process. Do your child a favor and shield him from filling his mind with useless or harmful memories. Help him to fill his memory instead with a beauty that will support him on his journey toward God.

Forming a Catholic Intellect

Before turning to your child's prayer life, I'd like to say a few words about teaching the phlegmatic. I am including some general suggestions for homeschool parents and classroom teachers.

Cheating can be an issue for this child. He might forget to do his homework, then lie that he misplaced his notebook. He might neglect to study, and find his eyes straying to his neighbor's test paper. Emphasize that virtue is more important than perfect grades. Let him know it's okay to make mistakes, okay to forget sometimes. Gently suggest ways he can overcome these weaknesses rather than shaming him for being absent-minded or for getting bad grades.

You can help him remember to do his homework each day by scheduling a consistent time and place for it. His siblings can study at the same time. Give him a checklist for bringing books home from school or finishing his homeschool assignments. Forming the habit of being more organized with his work will take time and patience. He can easily forget the same activities day after day.

The phlegmatic works slowly, but will usually finish his work if given enough time. When teaching a new skill, break it down into small steps and work on one at a time. Complex math problems, for example, may immobilize him until he has mastered each step in order. Lots and lots of practice helps. Rather than overloading him with directions, try to keep it simple. Give some basic instruction, then let him practice. Repeat daily until it becomes second nature.

Some pure phlegmatics put so little mental energy into their work, they do not really learn, even after weeks of practice. You might find that he completely forgets how to do long division, for example, after a week of working on something else. Be patient. Be willing to let him progress slowly. The phlegmatic may be very intelligent, but he must be able to choose his pace. Of course, as with all temperamental weaknesses, you will have to challenge him more as he gets into junior high and high school. He has to learn to adapt himself to the expectations of teachers and future employers. He must grow up. But don't be dismayed if he is somewhat behind where your other children were at the same grade in elementary school. Try to find the balance between coddling him and having unrealistic expectations.

CHAPTER 11

Prayer Development for the Phlegmatic

P ast popes have minced no words in speaking about the role
of parents regarding prayer. For example, Pope St. John Paul
II wrote:

The concrete example and living witness of parents is fundamen-
tal and irreplaceable in educating their children to pray. Only by
praying together with their children can a father and mother—
exercising their royal priesthood—penetrate the innermost depths
of their children's hearts and leave an impression that the future
events in their lives will not be able to efface. Let us again listen to
the appeal made by Paul VI to parents: "Mothers, do you teach
your children the Christian prayers? Do you prepare them, in
conjunction with the priests, for the sacraments that they receive
when they are young: Confession, Communion and Confirmation? Do you encourage them when they are sick to think of
Christ suffering, to invoke the aid of the Blessed Virgin and the
saints? Do you say the family rosary together? And you, fathers,
do you pray with your children, with the whole domestic community, at least sometimes? Your example of honesty in thought
and action, joined to some common prayer, is a lesson for life, an
act of worship of singular value. In this way you bring peace to

your homes: *Pax huic domui.* Remember, it is thus that you build up the Church."[69]

Prayer is at the heart of the spiritual life, no matter what age a person is. The most important prayer is the Holy Mass. Your faithful attendance at Mass on Sundays and Holy Days of Obligation, as well as your active participation in the liturgy, show your child the importance of the Church's prayer. Study together the different parts of the Mass, the meaning of the words of the Creed, and some of the common Latin phrases used—even if you attend Mass in English.

Stages of Prayer Development

Saints Teresa of Avila and John of the Cross are Doctors of the Church regarding prayer. Teresa's masterpiece on prayer, *Interior Castle,* provides the foundation for the Catholic understanding of stages of prayer. Since we are speaking about children, we don't need to concern ourselves with contemplative prayer here. Contemplative prayer is a gift God gives to those who have made a great deal of progress in their spiritual lives. But we should understand the two types of prayer that we can pray with ordinary grace. They are vocal and mental prayer.

Vocal prayer uses words composed by someone else. The Our Father, Hail Mary, and Table Blessing are three of the first prayers children learn. Unfortunately, most instruction in prayer stops here. Many people teach their children to recite memorized prayers, but not what it means *to pray.*

Did you know that the Rosary is meant to be a means of meditating on the life of Christ? Although this may seem obvious to you, it is not obvious to children. If they try to focus on God during the

---

[69] *Familiaris Consortio,* no. 60.

Rosary, they will probably focus on thinking about the words of the prayers, rather than the mysteries. The Rosary is the perfect way to teach children to begin meditating on the life of Christ. The Rosary prayed well easily moves into mental prayer.

What is mental prayer? Mental prayer is communicating with God from the heart. It can take many forms, from a simple, *Thank you, Jesus,* when something goes well to sitting silently in God's presence.[70]

> Of all the different types of mental prayer, meditation on Sacred Scripture holds a special place.
>
> Meditation engages thought, imagination, emotion, and desire. This mobilization of faculties is necessary in order to deepen our convictions of faith, prompt the conversion of our heart, and strengthen our will to follow Christ. Christian prayer tries above all to meditate on the mysteries of Christ, as in lectio divina or the rosary. This form of prayerful reflection is of great value.[71]

In other words, meditating on Scripture teaches your child about Christ, while inspiring him to love and follow Christ. It engages his whole soul. The Catechism speaks powerfully about children and prayer:

> The catechesis of children... aims at teaching them to meditate on the Word of God in personal prayer, practicing it in liturgical prayer, and internalizing it all in order to bear fruit in a new life.[72]

Phlegmatics and Mental Prayer

The phlegmatic child, with his comfort with forms and rules, is often drawn to vocal prayers.[73] Teach him to enter into a more inti-

---

[70] Please note: I am not promoting Centering Prayer here. Please see my book *Is Centering Prayer Catholic?* for the problems with this method.
[71] CCC, no. 2708.
[72] CCC, no. 2688.

mate conversation with Christ through the Rosary. Begin teaching the prayers of the Rosary in the preschool years. The best way to go about this is by praying the Rosary regularly as a family. Each child should have his own set of Rosary beads.

From even the earliest days, give your child a book of pictures he can look at as he prays. Kathryn Marcellino has produced a beautiful Rosary coloring book that is inspired by the masters. Other coloring books are available free online. Your child can color his own book, then use it for something to look at as you pray together. By doing this he learns that the Rosary is about the lives of Mary and Jesus. He gets to know the stories before he understands the meaning of the names of the mysteries. Even adults can use pictures as a form of meditation. St. Teresa of Avila recommended this practice to cloistered nuns.

The Rosary creates a bridge between vocal and mental prayer. It provides a first taste of meditation on the Gospels. Later in this chapter I share a method of meditation on Sacred Scripture that I developed for my children. Teach the phlegmatic the method by using these twenty Scripture passages that correspond to the mysteries of the Rosary as follows. I have chosen to stay with Luke and Acts wherever possible, so that the child may get to know one writer's works in depth.

The Joyful Mysteries

1. The Annunciation—Lk 1:26-38
2. The Visitation—Lk 1:39-56
3. The Nativity—Lk 2:6-20
4. The Presentation in the Temple—Lk 2:22-38
5. The Finding of the Child Jesus in the Temple—Lk 2:41-52

---

[73] Bennetts, 228.

The Luminous Mysteries

1. The Baptism of the Lord—Jn 1:29-34
2. The Wedding at Cana—Jn 2:1-11
3. The Proclamation of the Kingdom—Lk 4:14-21
4. The Transfiguration—Lk 9:28-36
5. The Institution of the Eucharist—Lk 22:14-20

The Sorrowful Mysteries

1. The Agony in the Garden—Lk 9:39-53
2. The Scourging at the Pillar—Lk 23:6-16
3. The Crowing with Thorns—Mt 27:27-31
4. The Carrying of the Cross—Lk 23:26-32
5. The Crucifixion—Lk 23:33-49

The Glorious Mysteries

1. The Resurrection—Lk 24:1-12
2. The Ascension into Heaven—Acts 1:6-12
3. The Descent of the Holy Spirit—Acts 2:1-12
4. The Assumption of Mary—Rev 11:12-12:1
5. The Coronation—Rev 12:1-16

The phlegmatic child often has a vivid imagination. His interior world is more real to him than the world of his senses. This makes meditation relatively easy for him once he learns how to do it. However, two problems may occur. First, he can become lazy in prayer. Help him form the habit of reading Sacred Scripture as a starting point for his meditations. Otherwise, he can become aimless in his prayer, falling into daydreaming and stream of consciousness ramblings instead of real interaction with Jesus. The second possible problem is never moving beyond imagining scenes of Christ's life to thinking about what he can learn from them and talking to God about them. His prayer can thus become a kind of "holy make-believe." He could easily fall into the trap of imagining himself doing great deeds for God, instead of letting God make real, difficult changes in his heart.

The phlegmatic has the tendency to do the minimum he can get by with. This can affect his prayer life as well. If he is a moral person who goes to Church on Sunday and tries to do what is right, he might not see the need for daily mental prayer. Isn't he doing fine without it? For other temperaments, you can point out how relationships take work and need regular communication. This may not convince the phlegmatic. He gets by with minimal engagement with his family and friends. He is content to listen, not giving much input. Since he is loyal, he does not easily understand that others may not be loyal too—especially when he seems detached from the relationship.

As with so many things, habits formed in youth can really help here. If you as a family set aside daily time for mental prayer (rather than just requiring it of your child), it will become part of his identity. He will find it difficult to imagine life without daily prayer. Also, appeal to the love Christ has for him. Assign him meditations on the Passion—or compassion—of Jesus. Hang images of the Good Shepherd carrying a lamb, Jesus relating to children, or other works of art that show his goodness and tenderness, on the walls of your home.

Recently we as a family have each noted what we are grateful for around the dinner table each night. This practice helps the phlegmatic take notice of the little graces that God gives him throughout the day, the little ways God shows his love. A phlegmatic who understands the love of Christ will want to reciprocate it. Encourage him to speak to Jesus throughout the day, especially when he is having a hard time or needs support. Let Jesus become the knight that comes to his rescue. Let Jesus be his champion. He will always strive to love the one who has been so good to him. He will want to spend time with the Lord out of gratitude and affection.

Finally, give the phlegmatic help for overcoming distractions in prayer. Share how you fight distractions.

Art and Laraine Bennett suggest that phlegmatics keep a prayer journal.[74] This is a practice that comes from St. Ignatius' Exercises, where he encouraged his followers to reflect on their prayer times. A journal should not be used during prayer, but after it. Your phlegmatic teen can use this in conjunction with the method of meditation that follows. Have him write down the insights he receives from reflecting on the Scriptures, any sins he repented of, inspirations, and resolutions. This journaling could replace the worksheet for meditation on the Gospels if you choose. Some phlegmatics may want to skip this step, just as they avoid making a grocery list or other reminders for themselves. If you can help your child form a habit of this type of journaling, it can help him to always seek to pray better and to remember what he should be working on. It can also help him know what he needs to confess.

A Graduated Meditation Method for Children

In our homeschool, we use the Golden Children's Bible as a basis for unit studies. Each unit ends with a guided meditation on the text. I created the meditations myself. I have posted a few of these on my blog. I have also included some in the next chapter that I think are most helpful to the phlegmatic. Start with the meditation on Mary and Martha in the section below called "Learning to Use a Guided Meditation." This example uses both a passage of Scripture and a religious painting for meditation. Discussing and reflecting on reli-

---

[74] Bennetts, 246.

gious paintings can also be a starting point for meditation. Sometime in the future I hope to publish an entire book of the meditations I have made for my children.

We start doing these meditations in kindergarten. At that level, walk your child through every step of the prayer. As he becomes more practiced in it, give him greater freedom in the final section of the prayer, letting him converse with God in his own words instead of repeating mine or yours. I have included examples of both variations for the meditations in this book.

By ages ten to twelve, depending on the child, he should be able to begin creating his own meditations with a little help from you. If your child is in this age group or older and has never experienced a guided meditation, spend some time practicing that first. For the more experienced child or for a teen, encourage him to use his mind and imagination to read and ponder the Scriptures, then spend about five minutes praying about the passage.

In chapter 12, I provide a detailed example of prayer for older children, using the story of Jesus' baptism from Mark's Gospel, beginning in the section called "Meditation on the Gospels." A template for your child to use follows it. Make as many copies as you need for your family's use. Walk your child through the example first. Then, about once a week, practice with him on another Scripture passage, using the template. After doing this a few times, give him the template and have him practice on his own. Review what he wrote and clarify any part he did not understand. It took my two oldest children, then ages ten and twelve, a couple of times working on their own to fully understand the method.

Continue practicing the method this way once a week for three to five weeks. By then he will probably be ready for the next step. If he is not ready yet, let him continue as he has been doing until he is comfortable moving on.

The next step is to start simplifying the process, making it more of a prayer and less of a worksheet. He begins with the Sign of the Cross and an invocation to the Holy Spirit to guide him. Instead of writing down the sights and sounds in step 2, this time he simply imagines the scene for a few minutes. Then he continues on as before.

Once again, let him practice this for several weeks before moving on. Then he lists just one idea in step 3 and does step 4 in his head. He should try to make the entire prayer about ten minutes long, concentrating on the final step, which is the most important—conversing with God. If he runs out of things to say, he can return to the Scripture passage and find another idea to reflect (that is, meditate) on. He can also talk to God about other concerns. He should wait to write anything down until after he is done praying.

Finally, after about a year's practice with the method, he can extend his prayer time to fifteen minutes. Each subsequent year he should try to pray about five minutes longer, so that by the time he reaches adulthood, he is praying for thirty minutes at a time. The conversation (step 5) should be the part that is getting longer, not necessarily the reading or reflecting.

Remember, each child will advance at his own pace. Your phlegmatic will probably need more practice than some of your other children.

CHAPTER 12

Meditations to Use with Your Child

This chapter contains the meditations and templates I wrote about in chapter 11. Feel free to make copies of these prayers and templates for your family's use.

Learning to Use a Guided Meditation

1. Read aloud to your child Luke 10:38-42, using your favorite children's Bible.

2. Study the painting above.

It's Christ in the House of Martha and Mary, attributed to Georg Friedrich Stettner (courtesy of Wikimedia Commons). Ask your child to identify the people in the painting. Discuss the painting in this manner:

1. Martha and Mary are both holding something. What do you think those objects are? What does each represent? Mary is reading the Bible. This represents meditating on Sacred Scripture. Martha is holding a duck, symbolizing being busy with household tasks.

2. Who are the other people in the picture? A servant and probably some of the apostles.

3. What are they doing? Cooking, sitting at the table waiting for dinner, talking together.

4. How many people appear to have been listening to Jesus? Only Mary does.

5. Does Mary look disturbed by what Martha is saying? No, she looks peaceful.

6. Why do you think the artist filled the foreground/front of the picture with food? To show how much work Martha had to do or had been doing.

7. Do you think Martha was doing something important? Yes, Jesus and his apostles needed to eat.

8. What could she have done differently so she could sit and listen to Jesus too? She could have made a simpler meal.

3. Remind your child of the Feeding of the Five Thousand.

Summarize the story for him if necessary. Ask:

1. How much food did Jesus need to feed all those people? *Five loaves of bread and two fish.*

2. Do you think Martha needed to work all day to cook for Jesus? *Probably not, because he could have fed everyone miraculously, as he had done before.*

3. Why do you think Martha was working so hard? *She was probably trying to show Jesus how much she loved him by making him a great meal.*

4. Only one thing is needed.

Discuss:

1. What is the best way to show Jesus we love him? Listening to him and spending time with him, as Mary did.

2. How can we sit at Jesus' feet today? Go to Mass, read the Bible, and pray.

3. Jesus said only one thing was needed. What is this one thing? Spending time with God.

5. Lead your child in prayer.

Make the Sign of the Cross, then have your child close his eyes and picture the painting in his mind. This time, he is sitting at Jesus' feet in Mary's place.

For a child about age eight or older say: "Imagine what Jesus would say to you as you sat with him. What would you say back? Speak to Jesus now in your heart, just as you would speak if you were sitting at his feet." For a younger child, skip down to the final paragraph.

Sit in silence for a few minutes, with the length of time depending on your child's age. Stop before he gets too uncomfortable.

Then pray this prayer phrase by phrase, and let him repeat it (or read it with you for ages ten and older):

"Dear Jesus, I know you are with me, just as you were with Mary and Martha. You visit me in the Eucharist. You love me and watch over me at every moment. Thank you that we can speak to you just as Mary could. Help me always to listen to you. Teach me to pray to you from my heart every day. Never let me get too busy to spend time with you. I love you, Jesus. Be with me always. Amen."

More Guided Meditations for Phlegmatics

For each of the meditations that follow, read and discuss the Bible stories before using the prayer. Make sure your child understands the stories. Discuss any difficult words or concepts. Make sure you discuss the ideas that are incorporated into the prayer. Each has a variation for the younger child [Level 1] and for the child more experienced in meditative prayer [Level 2]. Feel free to adapt the meditations to fit your child's interests and struggles. You read the first part of the prayer aloud, pausing where indicated. Then you read the second part, phrase by phrase, letting a young child repeat the prayer.

Gideon Prayer (Jgs 6-8)

Close your eyes and imagine you are Gideon. You are a man from an unimportant family, a man who does not think of himself as brave or strong, yet an angel has appeared to you and told you to fight the Midianites. You obey the Lord and win. You do not want to rule the people. You know God has won the victory. All you desire is for your people to live in the peace God has won. [Pause]

Now imagine that two of your family members are arguing. You think you know who is right and who is wrong. You feel like arguing on the right side, but you realize that could make the situation worse. Instead, you try to help them find a compromise and stop fighting, so the house can be peaceful again. [Pause]

[Level 1] Heavenly Father, thank you that we do not have to solve all our problems by ourselves. You are always there to help us do the right thing. Bring peace to our family. Help me to follow your way, the way of peace, so that I may be your true child. Amen.

[Level 2] In your own words, ask God to guide you in becoming a peacemaker among your family and friends. [Pause for several minutes or as long as appropriate.] Amen.

Ruth Prayer (Ruth 1)

Close your eyes and imagine you are Ruth. Your husband and father-in-law have died, and your mother-in-law is alone. She is growing old and has no means to take care of herself. She is homesick for her own country and wants to go back. You know that if you go with her, you will be in a strange land, with new customs, a God you do not know, and your own parents will be far away. But you love Naomi. When you married her son, you chose to become part of her family, so you choose now to remain loyal to her. [Pause]

Now imagine that a new family has moved into the neighborhood. They have children your age. They come over often to play with you. You enjoy spending time with them, but they do not like your old neighbors (or friends). You feel like you can't play with _____ when your new friends are here. You decide to tell your new friends what great people _____ are. You say you can only be their friends if they are kind to your old friends as well. [Pause]

[Level 1] Lord Jesus, you are our model for friendship and loyalty. You were always loyal to God your Father, and you gave up your life out of love for us. Help me to be the kind of friend that you were. Help me to speak up for my friends, even when it is hard. Through the prayers of Ruth and Naomi, teach me to make sacrifices for those that I love. Amen.

[Level 2] In your own words thank Jesus for being your loyal friend. Ask him to help you always be loyal, even when it is difficult. [Pause for several minutes or as long as appropriate.] Amen.

Samson Prayer (Jgs 15)

Close your eyes and imagine you are Samson. You are alone, when suddenly a group of Philistines surrounds you and tries to capture you. You know that God has given you great strength in order to defeat the enemies of Israel. You say a quiet prayer, then pick up the only weapon near—the jawbone of a donkey. You feel the power of God surging through you, as you use the jawbone to fight off the Philistines. [Pause]

Now imagine that it is chore time. You do not feel like working hard. You recognize that your desire to disobey Mom and Dad is your enemy. You must defeat it, in order to grow into a strong man (or woman) of God. You say a quiet prayer for God to help you do what is right. Like Samson, you feel God's power within you, giving you the desire and the energy to do God's will. [Pause]

[Level 1] Heavenly Father, thank you for giving us the example of Samson, to teach us that all true strength comes from you. Help me to work hard to fight the enemy inside of me, which would keep me from doing your will. Let me never be blind to my own weaknesses, or think I can be strong on my own. Amen.

[Level 2] In your own words, talk to God the Father about Samson. Ask him for the strength to work hard, even when you don't want to. [Pause for several minutes or as long as appropriate.] Amen.

The Calling of the First Apostles (Matthew 4:18-22)

Close your eyes and imagine you are a fisherman. You sit in a small fishing boat near the shore of a still lake. The smell of fish surrounds you. With you are your father and brother. Your net is across your lap and you are preparing it for the day's catch. Suddenly you hear someone call your name. You look up. Jesus stands on the shore. He is calling you and your brother to be his followers. You glance at your brother and the two of you nod to each other. Then you hop into the shallow water and join Jesus without looking back. [Pause]

Now imagine that you are at Mass. Sitting during the first reading, your mind wanders to your favorite movie. You smile as you think of your favorite scene. Suddenly something tugs at your heart. You know you should be paying attention at Mass. You realize God is calling you to learn from him. You are tempted to keep daydreaming, to think about God later. But you remember the example of James and John and turn your mind immediately to God. [Pause]

[Level 1] Dear Jesus, it is hard to think of you every time I pray and all through Mass. When my mind wanders, please call me back. Help me listen to your voice and follow you at once.

[Level 2] In your heart, tell Jesus how much you long to be his disciple. Ask him for the grace to pay attention during your prayers, especially at Mass, and to listen to his voice in your heart throughout the day. [Pause for several minutes or as long as appropriate.] Amen.

Meditation on the Gospels

1. Read a small section of the Gospels.

First, choose one of the four Gospels to pray through from beginning to end. Then choose from it a passage of ten to twenty verses. For this example, we're using Mark 1:1-11. Read it silently and slowly.

2. Use your senses.

Record the sights, sounds, smells, et cetera, that you would encounter if you were present when this story took place. Brainstorm as many as you can think of. Here are a few for our example:

1. John's camel-hair clothing
2. the sound of running water
3. crowd noise

3. Look for a lesson.

What can you learn from this passage? Look for insight into Jesus' character, instruction in the faith, or practical spiritual help. List at least two or three lessons. Here are some possibilities:

1. Before Jesus comes to us, we must prepare our hearts.
2. John considered himself unworthy to untie Jesus' sandals.
3. Jesus will baptize with the Holy Spirit.
4. God is Father, Son, and Holy Spirit.
5. The Father is pleased with Jesus.

4. What does this mean?

Circle one of the lessons from step 3 to focus on. What does it mean to you? How can you apply it to your life? Why does it matter? We will use #1: Before Jesus comes to us, we must prepare our hearts.

> How can you prepare the way for Jesus in your heart? *You can be ready to do whatever God asks of you.* Is God asking anything of you right now that you are resisting? Is he calling you to give up any sin or attachment that you don't want to let go of? Have you been resisting his grace in any way?

Since this step tends to be very personal, write down two or three questions like these you are asking yourself, rather than the answers to the questions (so you can share the meditation with your parents or teacher). Answer them in your mind.

5. Talk to God.

Talk to God about your reflections. Ask him to send the Holy Spirit to help you. If necessary, ask for forgiveness. Make resolutions and tell God what you intend to do.

Example:

> Father in Heaven, I want to make my heart ready for your Son, Jesus, to come to me. Please send me your Spirit to give me strength. I know you are asking me to _____ and it's hard for me to do. Please forgive me for not obeying you recently. Change my heart so I am eager to obey you. I promise to use the grace that you are giving me to overcome temptation. Thank you for your aid. Amen.

Meditation on the Gospel

Name_____ Date_____

1. Choose a passage of 10 -20 verses. _____

2. Use your senses.

Record the sights, sounds, smells, tastes, and (physical) feelings you would encounter if you were present when the story took place.

_____

_____

_____

_____

3. Look for a lesson.

What can you learn from this passage? List three ideas that show insight into Jesus' character, instruction in the faith, or practical spiritual advice. _____

_____

_____

_____

4. What does this mean?

Circle one of the lessons from number 3 to focus on. What does it mean for you? How can you apply it to your life? Why does it matter? Since this step tends to be very personal, write down two or three questions like these that you are asking yourself, rather than the answers to the questions (so you can share the meditation with your parents or teacher). _____

_____

_____

_____

5. Talk to God.

Talk to God about your reflections. Ask him to send the Holy Spirit to help you. If necessary, ask for forgiveness. Make resolutions and tell God what you intend to do.

CHAPTER 13

Checklists

Saints and Heroes for Your Phlegmatic Child to Imitate

Please note that I am not recommending that your child imitate all aspects of the lives of the people here, only the positive ones! Problematic behavior from some of these famous people can generate great conversations with your phlegmatic child.

Abraham

Nehemiah

Hannah

Abigail

Esther

St. Barnabas (phlegmatic-melancholic)

St. Timothy

St. Gregory Nazianzen (phlegmatic-sanguine)

St. Theodosius of Cappadocia

St. Thomas Aquinas

Bl. Fra Angelico

St. Alfonso Rodriguez

St. Faustina Kowalska (phlegmatic-melancholic)

Ven. Fr. Solanus Casey

Pope St. John XXIII (phlegmatic-sanguine)

Mr. Rogers

Phlegmatic Book List

The following list is organized by virtue, then age group. *BOV* and *MC* refer to stories found in William Bennett's *Book of Virtues* and *The Moral Compass*. Starred items are included in the lesson plans in Chapter 14.

Diligence

All Ages

"The Farmer and His Sons" by Aesop *(BOV)*

"The Salt Merchant and His Ass" by Aesop

"The Ants and the Grasshopper" by Aesop (BOV)

"Hercules and the Wagoner" by Aesop (BOV)

"Theseus and the Stone" (BOV)

Jacob and Rachel (Gn)*

Primary Grades

*"The Brownies" (MC)**

Little One Step by Simon James

The Little Engine That Could by Watty Piper

Mike Mulligan and His Steam Shovel by Virginia Lee Burton

All in a Day by Cynthia Rylant

Thank You, Mr Falker by Patricia Polacco

The Boy Who Invented TV by Kathleen Krull

Middle Grades

Stone Fox by John Reynolds Gardiner

Carry On, Mr. Bowditch by Jean Lee Latham

Junior High and Older

Where the Lilies Bloom by Bill and Vera Cleaver

Little Women by Louisa May Alcott

Expressing Emotion and Affection

All Ages

"The King and His Hawk" by James Baldwin *(BOV)*

Primary Grades

The Way I Feel by Janan Cain

I'll Always Love You by Hans Wilhelm

When Sophie Gets Angry... Really, Really Angry by Molly Bang

Middle Grades

What to Do When Your Temper Flares: A Kid's Guide to Overcoming Problems with Anger by Dawn Huebner and Bonnie Matthews

Adapting to Change or Disappointment

All Ages

Beautiful Oops! by Barney Saltzberg

Black Beauty by Anna Sewell (great family read-aloud)

Primary Grades

We Are Best Friends by Aliki

Madame Martine by Sarah S. Brannen

Joseph Had a Little Overcoat by Simms Taback

Nine for California by Sonia Levitin

Middle Grades and Older

Anne of Green Gables by L. M. Montgomery

The Door in the Wall by Marguerite De Angeli

Overcoming Fear and Worry

All Ages

The Talking Eggs by Robert D. San Souci

The Bravest of Us All by Marsha Diane Arnold

Pegasus by Marianna Mayer

The Butterfly by Patricia Polacco

Preschool

Owl Babies by Martin Waddell

Primary Grades

The Kissing Hand by Audrey Penn

Jenny is Scared: When Sad Things Happen in the World by Carol Shuman

Ira Sleeps Over by Bernard Waber

The Invisible Boy by Trudy Ludwig

Brave Irene by William Steig

The Courage of Sarah Noble by Alice Dagliesh

Back of the Bus by Aaron Reynolds

Middle Grades

"Sojourner Truth," from *The Narrative of Sojourner Truth, 1875*

http://sandstreams.com/haven/character/courage/cgstory4.htm)

The Secret Garden by Frances Hodgson Burnett

Number the Stars by Lois Lowry

The Breadwinner by Deborah Ellis

Call It Courage by Armstrong Sperry

Junior High and Older

The Red Badge of Courage by Stephen Crane

The True Confessions of Charlotte Doyle by Avi

Honesty and Sincerity

All Ages

The Honest Farmer by Ella Lyman Cabot

The Emperor's New Clothes by Hans Christian Anderson*

Primary Grades

A Day's Work by Eve Bunting

A Promise is a Promise by Robert Munsch

Horton Hatches the Egg by Dr. Seuss

The Empty Pot by Demi*

Middle Grades
Shiloh by Phyllis Reynolds Naylor
Sam, Bangs and Moonshine by Evaline Ness
Juan Verdades: the Man Who Couldn't Tell a Lie by Joe Hayes

Junior High and Older
"Nobility" by Alice Carey (poem)

Books with Phlegmatic Main Characters

All Ages
Snowflake Bentley by Jacqueline Briggs Martin

Preschool
"Slowly, Slowly, Slowly," Said the Sloth by Eric Carle
The Story of Ferdinand by Munro Leaf

Primary Grades
Winnie the Pooh by A. A. Milne
Frog and Toad Are Friends by Arnold Lobel

Middle Grades and Older
King of Colors: The Story of Fra Angelico by Brother Roberto

High School
David Copperfield by Charles Dickens*
Daniel Deronda By George Eliot
Washington Square by Henry James
Brideshead Revisited by Evelyn Waugh
The Maiden's Bequest by George MacDonald and Michael Phillips
Persuasion by Jane Austen

Bible Verses for the Phlegmatic Child

Note: All the verses below are from the Revised Standard Version. Feel free to change grammar to fit contemporary standards (such as changing *every one* to *everyone)* or use another translation of your choosing.

These passages are perfect for phlegmatics to read and ponder: Luke 9:57-62, Luke 12:35-40, Matthew 25

Diligence

I hasten and do not delay to keep thy commandments. (Ps 119:60)

Go to the ant, O sluggard; consider her ways, and be wise. Without having any chief officer or ruler, she prepares her food in summer and gathers her sustenance in harvest. (Prv 6:6-8)

The hand of the diligent will rule, while the slothful will be put to forced labor. (Prv 12:24)

In all toil there is profit, but mere talk leads only to poverty. (Prv 14:23)

We must work the works of him who sent me while it is day; night comes, when no one can work. (Jn 9:4)

To those who by patience in well-doing seek for glory and honor and immortality, he will give eternal life. (Rom 2:7)

It is required of stewards that they be found trustworthy. (1 Cor 1:2)

And let us not grow weary in well-doing, for in due season we shall reap, if we do not lose heart. (Gal 6:9)

Look carefully then how you walk, not as unwise men but as wise, making the most of the time, because the days are evil. (Eph 5:15)

I can do all things in him who strengthens me. (Phil 4:13)

Whatever your task, work heartily as serving the Lord and not men, knowing that from the Lord you will receive an inheritance as your reward; you are serving the Lord Christ. (Col 3:23-24)

Be sober, be watchful. Your adversary the devil prowls around like a roaring lion, seeking some one to devour. Resist him, firm in your faith, knowing that the same experience of suffering is required of your brotherhood throughout the world. (1 Pet 4:8-9)

And we desire each one of you to show the same earnestness in realizing the full assurance of hope until the end, so that you may not be sluggish, but imitators of those who through faith and patience inherit the promises. (Heb 6:11-12)

Whoever knows what is right to do and fails to do it, for him it is sin. (Jas 4:17)

Expressing Emotion and Affection

For everything there is a season, and a time for every matter under heaven: ... a time to weep, and a time to laugh; a time to mourn, and a time to dance. (Eccl 3:1, 4)

Blessed are the merciful, for they shall obtain mercy. (Mt 5:7)

Do unto others as you would have them do unto you. (Mt 7:20)

Let love be genuine; hate what is evil, hold fast to what is good; love one another with brotherly affection; outdo one another in showing honor. (Rom 12:9-10)

Rejoice with those who rejoice, and weep with those who weep. (Rom 12:15)

Bear one another's burdens, and so fulfill the law of Christ. (Gal 6:2)

Overcoming Fear and Worry

In God I trust without a fear. What can man do to me? (Ps 56:11)

Fear not, for I am with you, be not dismayed, for I am your God; I will strengthen you, I will help you, I will uphold you with my victorious right hand. (Is 41:10)

For surely I know the plans I have for you, says the Lord, plans for your welfare and not for harm, to give you a future with hope. (Jer 29:11)

The fruit of the Spirit is love, joy, peace, patience, kindness, goodness, faithfulness, gentleness, self-control. (Gal 5:22)

Have no anxiety about anything, but in everything by prayer and supplication with thanksgiving let your requests be made known to God. And the peace of God, which passes all understanding, will keep your hearts and minds in Christ Jesus. (Phil 4:6-7)

For God did not give us a spirit of timidity but a spirit of power and love and self-control. (1 Tim 1:7)

Honesty and Sincerity

Now therefore fear the LORD, and serve him in sincerity and in faithfulness. (Jos 24:14)

O Lord, who shall sojourn in thy tent? Who shall dwell on thy holy hill? He who walks blamelessly, and does what is right, and speaks truth from his heart. (Ps 15:1-2)

Truthful lips endure forever, but a lying tongue lasts only a moment. (Prv 12:19)

Like clouds and wind without rain is a man who boasts of gifts he does not give. (Prv 25:14)

Whoever conceals his transgressions will not prosper, but he who confesses and forsakes them will obtain mercy. (Prv 28:13)

Simply let your 'Yes' be 'Yes,' and your 'No,' 'No'; anything beyond this comes from the evil one. (Mt 5:37)

The truth will set you free. (Jn 8:32)

Therefore, putting away falsehood, let every one speak the truth with his neighbor, for we are members one of another. (Eph 4:25)

Prayer

For where two or three are gathered in my name, there am I in the midst of them. (Mt 18:20)

CHAPTER 14

Lesson Plans

Feel free to adapt the following lessons to your child's age, sex, and interests. You can also use these lessons with all your children together, or even with a small homeschool co-op. Most of them are designed to be spread over several days.

Lesson Plan 1: Speaking Up for the Truth

Ages: 7-12

Objective: The child will learn to speak up for the truth.

Summary: The child will read and discuss *The Emperor's New Clothes* by Hans Christian Andersen. This will lead to a discussion on when one must speak up for the truth and when it is okay to remain silent. Copy work and an optional study on admonishing sinners follows.

Materials: *The Emperor's New Clothes* by Hans Christian Andersen
Bible
Lined paper and pen for copy work

1. Introducing the topic

Ask your child: Do you ever feel afraid to speak up for the truth? What kind of problems can you have when you decide not to keep quiet? *Hurting someone else's feelings, having others think you are a goody-goody, embarrassment, not being accepted by the group, etc.*

2. The Emperor's New Clothes

Read the story together. Discuss:
1. Why did the king believe the swindlers? *He believed his servants could see the cloth, so he thought the problem must lie with himself.*
2. Why didn't any of his ministers tell the truth? *They didn't want to be called unfit for office or stupid.*
3. Who finally told the king the truth? *A child.*
4. Why do you think he spoke up? *Kids don't think about what they are going to say but just blurt it out. He did not have anything to lose.*
5. What would you have done if you were one of the king's ministers? Be honest, now!

6. Why was it important for the king to hear the truth? *He was naked. How embarrassing and immodest!*

7. Brainstorm some ways that the ministers could have told the king the truth without getting into trouble.

3. Copy work

Have the child copy this Bible verse in his best handwriting:

"God did not give us a spirit of timidity but a spirit of power and love and self-control. Do not be ashamed then of testifying to our Lord." (2 Timothy 1:7-8)

Ask: What is *timidity?*
If the child cannot give a good definition, have him look it up in the dictionary, helping him as necessary for his age.

4. When is the truth necessary?

Explain to your child that although lying is always a sin, we don't always have to tell the truth. How can this be so? *Sometimes we can remain silent or avoid speaking directly.*
Read this list of situations with your child. Have him decide whether or not he should speak up in each situation. The older child (10-12 years) could write the situations in two columns, Speak and Keep Silent.

- Your sibling's hair is sticking up on the way into Church.
- You don't like the dinner your grandma is serving.
- You see your friend cheating on a test.
- A neighbor praises a politician that you know your parents don't like.
- Your classmate says a bad word.
- You feel sick when you get up in the morning.
- Your mom forgot that you lost some privileges for misbehavior.

- Your dad makes a statement about current events that you know is wrong.
- A bully is teasing a smaller child.
- A friend wears an ugly outfit.

Now talk about why it's right to keep silent in some of these situations and to speak out in others. Guide your child toward a standard of speaking up, including things such as: someone sins against you, another person is being hurt, you are being taken advantage of, it's a matter of faith or morals, etc.

Optional: Discuss how this story relates to the spiritual work of mercy of admonishing the sinner. Study one of the saints suggested in chapter 9 for this work of mercy.

For a series of worksheets and activities on *The Emperor's New Clothes* aimed at third graders, see

http://www.k12reader.com/worksheet/classic-literature-the-emperors-new-clothes/

Lesson Plan 2: Plant a Seed for Honesty

Ages: 6-10

Objective: The child will learn to act honestly, even under pressure.

Length of time: This lesson works well spread out over several days, with step 6 taking a number of weeks to complete.

Summary: Reading *The Empty Pot* by Demi leads to a discussion on telling the truth even when you are scared of the consequences. Then the child plants mystery seeds and waits for the flowers to grow and bloom as he practices honesty in daily life.

Materials: *The Empty Pot* by Demi
Bible
Lined paper and pen for copy work
Planter, potting soil, and snap dragon seeds (keep identity of seeds secret)

1. Introducing the topic

Discuss:

1.   What does it mean to be honest?
2.   Why is honesty important?

2. *The Empty Pot*

Read *The Empty Pot* together or have an older child read it on his own. Discuss:

1.   Why didn't Ping's flower grow? *The emperor had cooked the seeds.*
2.   Do you thing Ping was suited to be emperor? Why or why not? *Yes, because he was honest and persevering, and not afraid of embarrassment. He was also thoughtful and serious.*

3. Why do you think the other children tried to deceive the emperor? *They wanted to win the contest.*

4. When are you tempted to lie?

3. Copy work

Have your child copy John 8:32, "The truth will set you free," in his best manuscript or cursive hand. Hang the completed copy work in a place where he may be tempted to lie—the bedroom or classroom wall, for example.

4. When the truth can get you in trouble

Read Mark 14:26-72. Discuss:

1. What did Jesus predict about Peter? *He will deny Jesus three times.*

2. How did Peter react? *He insisted he would never do such a thing.*

3. What did Peter, James, and John do in the garden? *They fell asleep.*

4. How could praying have helped Peter? *God may have given him the grace to overcome his fear so that he would not deny Jesus.*

5. Is there anything else you would have done differently if you were Peter? *Answers will vary.*

6. How did Jesus act differently than Peter? *He admitted he was the Christ, even though he knew it meant he would be crucified.*

7. How do you think Jesus had the strength to be honest? *He spent time in prayer.*

8. What can you do when faced with the temptation to lie or cheat? *Pray, ask your guardian angel for help, walk away, etc.*

9. Did the Sanhedrin set Jesus free when he told the truth? *No.* What do you think John 8:32 means? *An older child can write his answer, as detailed and long as you deem appropriate for his age.*

5. Compare and contrast St. Peter and Ping from *The Empty Pot* (optional).

Make the comparison written or oral, as you choose.

6. Think ahead

Tell your child that fear can lead to lying. Have him make a list of his fears. Help him remember when any of those fears has led to lying. Has he lied to escape punishment for not finishing his work? So that he would be able to go out to play with his siblings or friends? In order to avoid an argument? So others wouldn't criticize him?

Think of situations where he could be tempted to lie in the future. What can he do to avoid the near occasion of sin? How can you help him?

7. Plant a seed

Give your child a "mystery" (snap dragon) seed to plant in a pot. Make it his responsibility to water and care for it. Challenge him to form a habit of telling the truth by the time the flowers bloom.

Optional: Predict when the shoot will appear, what type and color of flowers it will have, and when it will bloom. Observe and illustrate the different stages of the plant's growth.

Lesson Plan 3: Walking Toward Responsibility

Ages: 6-10

Objective: The child will form a new habit of diligent work.

Summary: After reading a traditional fairy tale, the child will work on making a new chore a habit. Doing it well without being reminded wins him extra treats. I call this lesson "Brownies for Brownies," because in *The Moral Compass* version the elves are called brownies.

Materials: *The Elves and the Shoemaker* by Jacob Grimm and Jim Lamarche (or use the version called "Brownies" in *The Moral Compass)*
Children's Bible
Bible verse to copy
Handwriting paper and pen
Your child's shoes
White construction paper
Scissors
Brownies or another special treat

Preparation: Write out Proverbs 14:23, "In all work there is profit," in manuscript or cursive for your child to copy.

1. *The Elves and the Shoemaker*

1. Read aloud. Discuss:
2. Why did the elves help the shoemaker? *He was a good and generous man who was in need.*
3. How did the shoemaker help the elves? *He and his wife made them clothes to wear.*

4. How can you be like the elves? *I can do work without being asked, in secret, etc.*

5. How do you think the shoemaker and his wife felt when they saw the shoes completed? *They were happy, relieved, etc.*

6. How do you think the elves felt when they saw their new clothes? *They were happy. They felt satisfied that their work was rewarded. They felt like they had completed their job, etc.*

2. Copy work

Have the child copy Proverbs 14:23 in his best manuscript or cursive hand, according to his age. Discuss:

1. How did the elves profit from their work? *They received new clothes.*

2. Do we always receive material goods/something we can see, touch, or hear when we work hard? *No.*

3. Then how is this verse true? *Sometimes our "profit" is the feeling of satisfaction we have for getting our work done and pleasing others, the lack of fear or shame for not completing our work. God will reward all our hard work in Heaven, especially work we do out of love. All work that is done out of love or obedience will bring us closer to God.*

3. Matthew 6:1-18

Read this passage aloud. Discuss:

1. Why did Jesus say we should do our good deeds in secret? *Then we are doing them for a reward from God, instead of praise from other people.*

2. What examples did Jesus give of things we should do in secret? *Praying, giving to the poor, fasting.*

3. Can you think of other things you could do in secret just to please God?

4. Walk towards your brownies.

Explain that your child will get a reward for doing a certain chore or chores without being reminded. Make a specific goal with him for earning brownies (or another special treat). How many chores must he do, or for how many days? He should complete his tasks without having to be reminded, like the elves who did their work in secret.

Trace the sole of your child's shoes on construction paper. Cut them out (or have your child do so) and use them as a pattern to make several pairs of soles. Write the name of a chore or a day of the week on each shoe. When the child finishes his chore, he can color one shoe. Feel free to use the shoes creatively. For example, you could cut them out and make footprints leading down the hall from the child's bedroom to the kitchen to indicate that keeping his room clean for a certain number of days without being asked will lead to brownies in the kitchen.

Note: Hugs and words of praise along the way can help your child maintain his momentum until he reaches his goal. Make sure you notice that he has done his work and tell him so.

Lesson Plan 4: Works of Love

Ages: 10-14

Objective: The child will form the habit of doing little tasks out of love.

Summary: After reading about Jacob working to marry Rachel, and a passage from the New Testament, the child will perform secret little acts of love for his family members.

Materials: Bible
Bible verse to copy (See calligraphic version below)
Good quality drawing paper
Calligraphic pen
Markers or colored pencils (Optional)

1. Jacob and Rachel

Read the story, found in Genesis 29, together or silently. Use a children's or adults' Bible as appropriate. Discuss:

1. What did Jacob offer to do so he could marry Rachel? *He would work for Laban for seven years.*

2. How did Jacob feel about working? *The time passed very quickly and he was happy to do it in order to gain Rachel.*

3. What happened at the end of seven years? *Laban tricked him and gave him his daughter Leah instead.*

4. How did Jacob eventually marry Rachel? *He worked an additional seven years for Laban.*

5. How do you think Jacob felt when he realized Laban had tricked him? *He probably felt angry and disappointed.*

6. Why was Jacob willing to work hard for so long? *He loved Rachel so much.*

7. Would you be willing to work for many years to be able to spend your life with someone you love?

2. Copy work

Have the child copy 1 John 3:18 in his best handwriting. You can have him do a calligraphic version, copying the one below, with a special pen. Then he can color in some details like a medieval illuminated manuscript. Display the finished work.

3. Matthew 6:1-18

Read the passage together. In this passage, Jesus talks about three actions being done in secret out of love for God. Have your child brainstorm secret acts of love he can perform for different family members over the next week. Encourage him to do as many as he can.

4. Final Discussion

Discuss:
1. How many secret acts of love did you perform?
2. Was it difficult to do them secretly? Did anyone catch you?
3. How did you feel when you performed them? How did you feel after a week of doing this?
4. What are some secret ways you can show love for God? How could you work for God as faithfully as Jacob worked for Rachel?

"Little children, let us love not in word or speech, but in deed and in truth."

– 1 John 3:18

Lesson Plan 5: Character Analysis of David Copperfield

Ages: 14-18

Objective: The student will learn from Charles Dickens' *David Copperfield* how to use his temperament for his and others' benefit.

Procedure: Add these questions to your child's study of *David Copperfield* or use them for a stand-alone character study.

1. The first line of the novel reads, "Whether I shall turn out to be the hero of my own life, or whether that station will be held by anybody else, these pages must show." How does this sentence highlight David's phlegmatic temperament? *The phlegmatic often feels he is overlooked or insignificant. He fears he won't reach his potential, that even his own life is controlled by others.*

2. What other characteristics of a phlegmatic do you see in David Copperfield? *He is kind and understanding. He rarely judges others, who sometimes take advantage of him. He is naive. He lets others continue doing evil without stopping them. He takes a long time to grow up. He is very focused on his writing and successful with it. He fails to think ahead and does not easily learn from past mistakes. He is loyal and usually obedient, but can flash out in anger now and then.*

3. How do David's phlegmatic shortcomings hurt him or others in the following situations?
    *   His flight from London to Dover? *He trusts a stranger to help him and has his money and possessions stolen so that he has to walk.*

- Uriah Heep's pursuit of Agnes Wickfield? *Although he bristles at the thought of Uriah pursuing Agnes, he does little to help her, preoccupied with his own affairs. He fears Uriah. He also probably believes, as Mr. Micawber does that "something will turn up" to foil Uriah's plans without David having to act.*
- David's relationship with Steerforth? *He brushes aside Steerforth's self-crticisms and refuses to see anything but good in him, despite evidence to the contrary. He lets Steerforth lead him along, having a sort of hero-worship for him.*

4. How does David use his temperament positively? Give one detailed example. *Possible examples: accepting Mr. Dick, focusing so much on his writing that he succeeds, his humility concerning his success, accepting Dora's weaknesses after his aunt talks to him, accepting the role his immaturity played in his marriage to Dora, accepting and having compassion for people of all walks of life.*

5. Dickens uses the term *phlegmatic* once in his book. Which character does he call phlegmatic? *Mr. Barkis.* Do you agree? *Yes. Mr. Barkis was content to let David do his wooing for him. Although he liked Pegotty, he did not approach her on his own. He did not want to face rejection. He was timid. He was also loyal and kind. He appreciated good cooking.*

6. What temperament do you think Clara Copperfield was? *Probably sanguine-phlegmatic.* What happened when Mr. And Miss Murdstone tried to change her temperament? *She fell into depression and eventually died.*

7. Choose one mistake that David made due to his temperament. How could he have acted differently? What advice would you give him, one phlegmatic to another? Be realistic about what he could do. *Answers will vary.*

CHAPTER 15

Templates

Teaching Your Phlegmatic Child Responsibility

"Three things are necessary for the salvation of man: to know what he ought to believe; to know what he ought to desire; and to know what he ought to do."

– St. Thomas Aquinas

Name_____ **Date**_____

Assess: Describe your child's work ethic.

_____
_____
_____
_____
_____
_____
_____
_____
_____
_____

Create goals: How would you like your child to grow in responsibility by the end of this year?

_____
_____
_____
_____
_____
_____
_____
_____
_____
_____

Choose methods and materials: How will you help your child towards these goals?

_____
_____
_____
_____
_____
_____
_____
_____
_____
_____
_____
_____
_____
_____
_____
_____
_____

Review: What progress did your child make in responsibility? Where does he still need to grow?

_____
_____
_____
_____
_____
_____
_____
_____
_____
_____
_____
_____
_____
_____

Teaching Your Phlegmatic Child Honesty

"Sweeping problems under the rug does not solve them."

– St. John Bosco

Name_____ **Date**_____

Assess: Describe your child's honesty.

_____
_____
_____
_____
_____
_____
_____
_____
_____
_____

Create goals: How would you like your child to grow in honesty by the end of this year?

_____
_____
_____
_____
_____
_____
_____
_____
_____
_____
_____
_____
_____
_____

Choose methods and materials: How will you help your child towards these goals?

_____

_____

_____

_____

_____

_____

_____

_____

_____

_____

_____

_____

_____

_____

_____

_____

_____

Review: What progress did your child make in honesty? Where does he still need to grow?

_____

_____

_____

_____

_____

_____

_____

_____

_____

_____

_____

_____

_____

Teaching Your Phlegmatic Child Make Decisions

"If any of you lacks wisdom, let him ask God, who gives to all men generously and without reproaching, and it will be given him."

– James 1:5

Name_____ **Date**_____

Assess: Describe your child's ability to make decisions.

_____
_____
_____
_____
_____
_____
_____
_____
_____
_____

Create goals: How would you like your child to grow in decision-making ability by the end of this year?

_____
_____
_____
_____
_____
_____
_____
_____
_____
_____
_____

Choose methods and materials: How will you help your child towards these goals?

_____
_____
_____
_____
_____
_____
_____
_____
_____
_____
_____
_____
_____
_____
_____
_____
_____
_____

Review: What progress did your child make in making decisions? Where does he still need to grow?

_____
_____
_____
_____
_____
_____
_____
_____
_____
_____
_____
_____
_____
_____

Teaching Your Phlegmatic Child to Overcome Fear

"Let nothing disturb you, let nothing frighten you, all things are passing away: God never changes."

– St. Teresa of Avila

Name_____ **Date**_____

Assess: Describe your child's tendency toward fear and timidity.

_____
_____
_____
_____
_____
_____
_____
_____
_____
_____

Create goals: How would you like your child to grow in confidence by the end of this year?

_____
_____
_____
_____
_____
_____
_____
_____
_____
_____
_____

Choose methods and materials: How will you help your child towards these goals?

_____

_____

_____

_____

_____

_____

_____

_____

_____

_____

_____

_____

_____

_____

_____

_____

_____

Review: What progress did your child make in overcoming fear? Where does he still need to grow?

_____

_____

_____

_____

_____

_____

_____

_____

_____

_____

_____

_____

_____

_____

Teaching Your Phlegmatic Child to Think About Others

"Find out how much God has given you and from it take what you need; the remainder is needed by others."

– St. Augustine

Name_____ Date_____

Assess: Describe your child's tendency to focus on himself.

_____
_____
_____
_____
_____
_____
_____
_____
_____
_____

Create goals: How would you like your child to grow in thinking more about others by the end of this year?

_____
_____
_____
_____
_____
_____
_____
_____
_____
_____
_____

Choose methods and materials: How will you help your child towards these goals?

_____

_____

_____

_____

_____

_____

_____

_____

_____

_____

_____

_____

_____

_____

_____

_____

_____

_____

Review: What progress did your child make in thinking about others? Where does he still need to grow?

_____

_____

_____

_____

_____

_____

_____

_____

_____

_____

_____

_____

_____

_____

Afterword

I trust that by now you have a better understanding of your phlegmatic child, his motivation, strengths, and weaknesses. You cannot force him to use his gifts. More than those of any other temperament, the phlegmatic must be motivated from within. But with the graces of holy matrimony, you and your spouse can help him experience God's love and desire to respond to it. You can be his models in prayer and virtue, teaching him to make a growing relationship with God his top priority in life. Once he has begun sailing down this river, he is unlikely to stop.

As your sister in Christ and a fellow parent striving to lead my children toward holiness, I will be praying for you and your child. When you are frustrated with his foibles, remember that God desires his spiritual growth even more than you do. He made your child to be a saint. Be patient. Be prayerful. Be loving. Be ready to share an eternity in heaven with this awesome gift God has given you—your phlegmatic child!

Phlegmatic Versus Supine

In the twentieth century some psychologists began to move away from the understanding that the temperaments were distinguished by patterns of reactions and impressions. In the 1950s Dr. William Schutz devised a personality test based on three characteristics: inclusion, control, and affection. Schutz rejected the idea that his test measured temperament or any inborn quality. He wanted to analyze more fluid characteristics. In fact, his way of looking at personalities had many similarities to the occult Enneagram. Schutz himself lived and taught for a time at the New Age Esalen Institute, (in)famous for syncretism. His test is known as the FIRO-B.

Despite these potential problems, Protestant psychologists Richard and Phyllis Arno began applying the FIRO-B to temperament studies. They developed their own test based on Schutz's system and gave it to thousands of patients. What emerged was an unexpected fifth pattern of answers. The Arnos believed this showed there are really five basic temperaments. In place of phlegmatic on the temperament square, they substituted the term *supine*. Then they used the term *phlegmatic* for people they said were neither introverts nor extroverts, but had a "neutral" temperament. Some of the traditional characteristics of the phlegmatic were split between this new neutral temperament and the old place on the square that was now called supine.

Obviously, there are problems with this view. The classic system does not allow for more than four basic patterns of behavior. One's reactions must be either quick or slow. One's impressions must either last or fade. The only other possibility is that sometimes one reacts quickly and other times slowly, or sometimes one holds onto impressions and other times lets them go. But these variations were already covered by the idea of temperament blends.

If you reject the understanding that the temperaments come from inborn reaction patterns, it would seem that you reject the understanding that they are biological or genetic. But the classic temperaments had always been seen as inborn and unchangeable, as opposed to adaptable personalities. The Arnos thought they found a solution to this dilemma. They coined the term "spiritual genetics." They began teaching that temperament is an aspect of the soul God breathes into each human, not part of the body. They subscribe to the common Protestant view that man is made up of body, soul, and spirit. As Richard Arno writes, "you are a spiritual being, you possess a soul and you live in a body."[75] Spiritual genetics do not come from one's parents, but directly from God. In that sense, they are not really genetic. But they are present from conception and cannot be changed any more than one's biological make-up. This is the Arnos' view.

Those who subscribe to the classic view of the temperaments believe that temperament is indeed biological, but the precise genes that determine temperament have not yet been discovered. They point to the prevalence of particular temperaments among certain

---

[75] Richard and Phyllis Arno, *The Missing Link: Revealing Spiritual Genetics* (Sarasota, FL: Peppertree, 2008), 51.

races of people as evidence that temperament is passed down from parent to child. My experience, for example, is that people of Japanese heritage tend toward a melancholic temperament, while southern Europeans tend toward choleric or sanguine temperaments.

The Arnos define temperament as something inborn, character as behavior learned as a result of one's environment, and personality as the mask one presents to the world. This is slightly different from most Catholic authors' understanding.

Here are some of the ways in which this new phlegmatic temperament is different from the classic view:[76]

New Phlegmatic	Classic Phlegmatic
May not necessarily have low energy, just doesn't use energy he has.	Has low energy by nature.
Task-oriented.	Loves people, but also needs time alone.
Only sleep rejuvenates him.	Time alone or "vegging" also rejuvenates him.
May try to inspire others, but remains uninvolved himself.	Leads by example. Gets involved in low-key, non-confrontational ways.
Has no fear of rejection.	Longs to be accepted.
Perfectionist.	Content with being "good enough."
Often hurts others with verbal defenses.	Careful of others' feelings, sometimes to a fault.
Rarely self-sacrificing.	Will do little loving tasks for those he feels close to.
Has lots of friends.	Liked by everyone, but often overlooked or forgotten.
Lacks self-motivation.	Can be very self-motivated in a few specific areas.
Judgmental.	Understands all sides.

---

[76] "Phlegmatic (Introvert)," *The Five Basic Temperaments,* http://fivetemperaments.weebly.com/phlegmatic.html (accessed December 31, 2015).

I find that the new twist on phlegmatic takes a considerably more negative view of this temperament than the classic one.

Here is a comparison of the supine with the classic phlegmatic:

Supine	Classic Phlegmatic
Over-sensitive, easily offended.	More easily offended for others than for himself, but it takes a lot to rattle him.
Has strong wishes and desires, but can't seem to voice them.	Doesn't voice feelings because he doesn't want to rock the boat or he simply doesn't understand his feelings.
Often considers others better than himself.	Can be honest about his shortcomings, but needs affirmation and encouragement.
Has great need for social interaction.	Likes people, but gets tired quickly in social situations.
Feels incapable of making good decisions.	Slow to decide because every choice appears equally good.
"Needs surface relationships."	Will accept flattery, but would prefer greater depths in friendships.
Will undertake many projects at once if they further relationships.	More than one or two projects at once can overwhelm him.
Both introverted and extroverted.	Introverted.

The Arnos say that the supine child is often tormented by other children. I suspect that what they take in adults to be temperamental characteristics may really be psychological reactions to deep hurts as children. The supine is supposed to be a sort of sanguine-melancholic mix. I doubt such a mix would be healthy. Nor do I believe that someone can truly be both introverted and extroverted. This would mean he is both inwardly focused and outwardly focused. I fail to see how he can really be both. The supine seems to be a conflicted person. He has been described as "codependent" and a "natural born victim."[77] Perhaps he is really a sanguine-phlegmatic, whose deep psychological wounds make him act like a victim and feel affronts more deeply than this temperament mix normally would. The Arnos have not convinced me that such a temperament exists, only that some people probably behave as they describe.[78]

All that said, I can understand why the confusion about the phlegmatic temperament exists. Art and Laraine Bennett say that the phlegmatic has the most complex and perplexing inner life of all the four temperaments.[79] Experts on the Myers-Briggs Type Indicator also identify phlegmatic mixes as complex and "puzzling."[80]

---

[77] Phyllis Pole Carter, PhD, *Temperament: Your Spiritual DNA (Your Master Key to Living in Significance)*, (iUniverse: 2004), 65.
[78] Author and temperament expert Laraine Bennett agreed with this assessment in an email exchange with me.
[79] Bennetts, 22.
[80] Renee Baron, *What Type Am I? Discover Who You Really Are* (1998: Penguin, NY), 139.

Bibliography

"10 Ways to Teach Your Children a Great Work Ethic," *All ProDad.* http://www.allprodad.com/10-ways-to-teach-your-children-a-great-work-ethic/(accessed December 31, 2015).

"All About Assertiveness," *Psychology Today.* https://www.psychologytoday.com/basics/assertiveness (accessed November 14, 2015).

Arno, Richard, and Phyllis Arno, *The Missing Link: Revealing Spiritual Genetics.* Sarasota, FL: Peppertree, 2008.

Aumann, Fr. Jordan, OP. *Spiritual Theology.* archive.org/stream/SpiritualTheologyByFr.JordanAumannO.p/AumannO.p.SpiritualTheologyall_djvu.txt (accessed April 12, 2015).

Baron, Renee. *What Type am I? Discover Who You Really Are.* New York: Penguin, 1998.

Bennett, Art, and Laraine Bennett. *The Temperament God Gave You: The Classic Key to Knowing Yourself, Getting along with Others, and Growing Closer to the Lord.* Manchester, NH: Sophia Institute Press, 2005.

Carter, Phyllis Pole, PhD, *Temperament: Your Spiritual DNA (Your Master Key to Living in Significance).* iUniverse: 2004.

Catechism of the Catholic Church (2nd ed.). Washington, DC: Libreria Editrice Vaticana-United States Conference of Catholic Bishops, 2000.

Groeschel, Benedict J. *Spiritual Passages: the Psychology of Spiritual Development.* New York: The Crossroad Publishing Co., 2004.

Hey Parents—Teach Them About Real Love! Parent Handbook on Human Sexuality. Diocese of La Crosse, Wisconsin, 2003.

Hock, Fr. Conrad. *The Four Temperaments and the Spiritual Life.* Milwaukee: The Pallotine Fathers, 1934. www.catholicapologetics.info/catholicteaching/virtue/temperaments.htm (accessed April 12, 2015).

John Paul II. *Familiaris Consortio,* Apostolic Exhortation on the Role of the Christian Family in the Modern World. Vatican Web site. November 22, 1981. w2.vatican.va/content/john-paul-ii/en/apost_exhortations/documents/hf_jp-ii_exh_19811122_familiaris-consortio.html (accessed April 12, 2015).

Kurcinka, Mary Sheedy. *Kids, Parents, and Power Struggles.* New York: HarperCollins, 2000.

LaHaye, Tim. *Spirit-Controlled Temperament.* La Mesa, CA: Post, 1992.

Littauer, Florence. *Personality Plus for Couples: Understanding Yourself and the One You Love.* Grand Rapids, MI: F. H. Revell, 2001.

Littauer, Florence. *Personality Plus for Parents: Understanding What Makes Your Child Tick.* Grand Rapids, MI: F. H. Revell, 2000.

McDonough, Tom. "Great Dads Foster Self-Confidence in Children," *Catholic Herald.* http://catholicherald.com/stories/Great-Dads-Foster-Self-Confidence-in-Children,4285. Jan. 10, 2001.

Nelsen, Jane, Lynn Lott & H. Stephen Glenn, "Lying," *Positive Discipline.* http://www.positivediscipline.com/articles/lying.html (accessed November 14, 2015).

"Phlegmatic (Introvert)," *The Five Basic Temperaments.* http://fivetemperaments.weebly.com/phlegmatic.html (accessed December 31, 2015).

Rowan, Chris, OTR, "The Impact of Technology on Child Sensory and Motor Development." *www.sensomotorische-integratie.nl/CrisRowan.pdf* (accessed April 12, 2015).

Seltzer, Leon F., PhD, "How—and How Not—to Stand Up for Yourself," *Psychology Today,* https://www.psychologytoday.com/blog/evolution-the-self/201209/how-and-how-not-stand-yourself (accessed November 14, 2015).

Acknowledgments

I thank God for all who have helped me with their work, prayers, and advice in writing and publishing this book, especially my husband, Dan Rossini; my children, who were the guinea pigs for the ideas and lesson plans; and the members of my GooglePlus Community, Indie Catholic Authors. This book is a tribute to your support and hard work on my behalf.

About the Author

Connie Rossini lives with her husband Dan in New Ulm, Minnesota, where she homeschools their four sons. She is the author of *Trusting God with St. Therese, Is Centering Prayer Catholic?* and *A Spiritual Growth Plan for Your Choleric Child.* She blogs on Carmelite spirituality and raising prayerful kids at contemplativehomeschool.com and is a columnist at SpiritualDirection.com. She also manages the Google Plus Community Indie Catholic Authors.